THE BEAUTY OF LISBON

ELÉCTRICO 28

A JOURNEY THROUGH HISTORY

NYSSE ARRUDA
TEXTO

CLARA AZEVEDO
FOTOGRAFIA

HENRIQUE CAYATTE
DESIGN

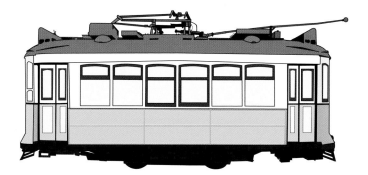

 TURISMO DE PORTUGAL

PUBLISHER
Imprensa Nacional-Casa da Moeda

AUTHOR
Nysse Arruda

PHOTOGRAPHY
Clara Azevedo

DESIGN, GRAPHICS AND LAYOUT
Henrique Cayatte Design
with Cristina Viotti and Pedro Gonçalves

TRANSLATION
Colin Archer

PRINTING AND FINISHING
Norprint

ISBN: 978-972-27-1889-9
Portuguese National Library No. 315 486/10
Print run 2000 copies

Lisbon, September 2010

This book is a sincere tribute to Lisbon, this marvellous city of colour and light, of hills and viewing terraces, this River Tagus with its waters of blue. It is a tribute to the city's history of thousands of years and the peoples who have been here and are here now.

It is also written in praise of one of the city's icons – Tram 28 – which runs through Lisbon's historic streets and squares, with the lulling effect of the ring of its bell on the daily lives of Lisbon people.

Much of the secret world of Lisbon, many of its monuments and the whole of its beauty are found on board the 28. As it rolls and sways over century-old rails, the life of this the city is maintained and renewed, its recollections are brought to life and the great figures of Portugal live once again.

The widest variety of people are also to be found on Tram 28, re-confirming Lisbon's centuries-long multicultural vocation. Tourists and Lisbon people, foreigners and the Portuguese, the rich and the poor share the beauty of Lisbon on hot summer days.

Through the open windows of Tram 28 waft the sweet smells of the gardens, the brilliant images of the jacarandas, and the breeze that ruffles the passengers' hair. Through the windows of the 28 the crystal-clear light of the sun can be seen bathing every street corner, every road and every building along the way, filling the perfect contours of Lisbon with colour.

Up the hills and down, the 28 pulsates with the vibrations of a beautiful city, an age-old landmark in a country that re-drew the map of the world with its fearless navigators.

NYSSE ARRUDA

A number of people deserve special thanks for the help they gave with this project from the very beginning: Maria Rui, who was instrumental in my meeting the photographer Clara Azevedo, the creator of the beautiful images in this book; the designer Henrique Cayatte, who created the original book cover and presented me to the historian José Sarmento de Matos, whose comments were a kind contribution to the final version of the book.

I should also like to express my special thanks to Dr. J. Manuel Silva Rodrigues, chairman of the board of Carris, and Dr. Luís Miguel Vale, general secretary of Carris, for their enthusiastic participation in the project and for the reception to launch the book in the Carris Museum in September 2010, and also to Dr. Estêvão de Moura, chairman of the board of Imprensa Nacional-Casa da Moeda, and to the editor in chief Duarte Azinheira who embraced this project without a moment's hesitation. And a special thanks to Tourism de Portugal. And, finally, a word of thanks to João Oliveira, who is in charge of the Casa Fernando Pessoa library, for his attention and his help in confirming information on the great Portuguese poet Fernando Pessoa.

To Lisbon and the Tagus, this beautiful river of blue, with its crystal-clear light.

How human was the metallic ring of the tram bell!

What a joyful landscape the simple rain in the street, rescued from the abyss!

Oh, Lisbon, my home!

"Trovoada", Bernardo Soares (Fernando Pessoa)

Fragment of the *Book of Disquiet*

This publication marks the starting point of a project that aims to inform the Portuguese and citizens from other countries about some of Portugal's most iconic places, which, on account of their particularities, it is important to publicise in a coherent manner.

The collection consists of a significant number of volumes. The first deals with a symbol of Lisbon that, in recent years, has captured the collective imagination as one of the city's greatest icons: Tram 28!

Lisbon has an umbilical relationship with its trams. Though limited today to a few lines, the trams once had an enormous network and criss-crossed the city from end to end. For years they were the preferred form of transport in the capital, until the advent of the "car culture". A President of the Republic (Teófilo Braga) took the tram to Belém Palace to carry out his noble duties as the country's highest official. There is no doubt that this image remains as an important marker of the influence of the trams on the life of the nation and its social life. Different times...

There are other trams than the one portrayed in the pages of this book. Though their routes are no less eclectic, they are less central and have not merited the same media treatment as the now famous "28": I mean Trams 15 and 18. These two lines travel to city locations considered of great beauty, historical importance and local symbolic significance.

A very great exponent of clean energy and a way of life that has disappeared, perhaps the trams should not have been withdrawn from the city in the way in which they were. They are part of the city of Lisbon and may even be the best way to get to know it: the Lisbon seen from a tram, for those who have already experienced it, is a different city. Not only because the sense of time is different but the trams themselves belong to a time of their own.

This book is a way of rediscovering a unique form of travelling through the city. INCM is honoured to have the opportunity to publish it – in two languages – not only as part of an important partnership with Carris and Turismo de Portugal but especially because of the marvellous work carried out by the team that produced it.

What else can the INCM wish those who buy this book than this: enjoy the discovery of the trams and have a good trip...?

ESTÊVÃO DE MOURA
CHAIRMAN OF THE BOARD OF IMPRENSA NACIONAL-CASA DA MOEDA

Tram 28 belongs to CARRIS. And to Lisbon, too.

When the author invited us to support this book, we assessed the project and decided to accept the invitation.

The publication of a book on Tram 28 is undoubtedly of great local and international interest, since 'the 28' is an inseparable part of Lisbon life and the city's image. There must be few Lisbon people who have never taken 'the 28' and felt the pleasure of seeing the city from a different angle.

The same happens with the great majority of visitors to our capital, who try out the unique way of seeing the city that 'the 28' provides.

'The 28' runs from Graça to Prazeres, via Baixa (the historic centre), Chiado and Estrela, offering a special way of seeing and perceiving everyday Lisbon and taking advantage of its light, its sounds and its smells.

Throughout its 137 years' history, CARRIS has always had one goal: to help to create high--quality forms of urban mobility, and thus develop a city with a better quality of life.

'The 28' is just one of the many routes contributing to this goal.

I hope this book helps to persuade you to experience 'the 28'.

And experience CARRIS.

Lisbon, September 2010

J. MANUEL SILVA RODRIGUES
CHAIRMAN OF THE BOARD OF CARRIS

I. From Baixa Pombalina to Lisbon Cathedral

Prazeres or Graça? Pleasures or Grace? These are the enchanting names of the destinations on offer at the Tram 28 stops on Rua da Conceição, in the Baixa (historic centre) of Lisbon, near Rua Augusta. Here, with the precise geometry of the streets traced out with the dynamism of the Marquis of Pombal after the 1755 earthquake, is the beginning of an unforgettable journey through Lisbon, its development over thousands of years, its views and its people. The history of Lisbon, one of the oldest cities in Europe, the second oldest capital in the European Union and the only European capital situated next to a nature reserve, in the Tagus estuary, spans over three millennia and, aboard Tram 28, the discovery begins...

Even before the typical 'ping-ping' of Tram 28 can be heard, it is most definitely worth making a visit to the ground floor of 9 Rua dos Correeiros, a street running directly parallel to Rua Augusta –

if it happens to be a Thursday (3-5 pm) or Saturday (10 am-1 pm and 3-5 pm). These are the days and times that the **Banco Millennium BCP Archaeological Nucleus (Núcleo Arqueológico do Banco Millennium BCP)** opens to the public and presents some of the city's most important archaeological finds from the last 2500 years. The cellar of the building, with its 'Pombaline' (mid-to-late 18th century) architecture stretches under the restored Portuguese mosaic for almost a whole block of Rua Augusta. It contains valuable archaeological remains that, on a journey back in time, reveal the development of Lisbon from the Ibero-Punic (from the 7th c. BC), Roman (1st c. BC-5th c. AD), Islamic (10th c. AD) and pre-Pombaline periods up to the reconstruction begun by the Marquis of Pombal after the 1755 earthquake.

Right at the entry, through a glass floor over a metal structure, it is possible to see the remains of a Roman road leading to the manufacturing units for fish preserves, next to the old waterfront area – large rectangular slabs retain the wheel marks of the Roman carts.

The main room of the Archaeological Nucleus also has a glass floor revealing a huge area with the remains of pre-Pombaline walls discovered during the 1991-1995 excavations when the building was being restored. It also contains various displays with different finds – pots, plates, amphorae, cups, water-pots, urns, knives, glasses, bowls, wooden bowls, jugs, jars, pans, mugs, tapered bowls, frying pans, picture fragments, and coins from the Punic, Roman, Islamic, medieval, Renaissance, pre-Pombaline and post-Pombaline periods.

The cellars are reached by a narrow wooden staircase and, by means of iron gangways suspended over the archaeological remains, another journey back in time begins. First there are the remains of a Punic house, confirming that Lisbon was a safe anchorage from the 7th c. BC, when Phoenician and Carthaginian merchants visited the place in search of precious metals.

Datable between the 5th and 2nd centuries BC, these rectangular houses had stone and clay bases that supported reed structures covered with fire-hardened clay. The centre of the house was occupied by a circle of rolled pebbles that served as a hearth for cooking.

The earliest Roman remains appear right at the side of the Phoenician remains – and next to the pine stakes put down to underpin the Baixa Pombalina after the earthquake – in an amalgam of different periods and overlapping floor levels. At the time, Lisbon was called Olisipo, a name attributed to the Phoenicians, though it is also loaded with legendary significance relating to the possible visit of the Greek hero Ulysses during his long journey back to Ithaca after the Trojan War. But the history of Lisbon goes back even further: it is one of the oldest cities in Europe, inhabited and visited for **over three thousands years**. Initially, there were Iron Age settlements (6th c. BC) and Iberian, Greek and (even in the 8th c. BC) Phoenician peoples, since Lisbon and the Tagus served as a support station for voyages to the British Isles, where the Phoenicians went in search of tin for the production of bronze.

Moreover, the Phoenicians and Carthaginians helped to develop Lisbon – which was under the control of Carthage at the time. From a commercial entrepôt on the northern maritime trade routes, the city turned into an important market where trading took place with the local tribes – in products such as metals, salted fish and salt from the region, and the predecessors of the present-day Lusitano horses, famous for their speed.

Even before the arrival of the Romans, Lusitanians occupied large swathes of the Iberian Peninsula. They produced a warrior, Viriato, who bitterly resisted the Roman conquerors. However, around 205 BC, after the conquest of Carthage, the people of Olisipo made a strategic alliance with the Romans and the city became part of the Roman Empire. In return, it gained the right to Roman citizenship for its inhabitants, a rare privilege at that time, and was renamed "Felicitas Julia".

From the 1st century BC – the time of Augustus – a significant Roman base for the preparation of fish products was set up in Lisbon, remaining in operation in the Tagus estuary until the end of the 4th century AD. The Roman salting tanks (cetaria, or large square stone containers where fish sauces were prepared) were built over the silting-up of the Ibero-Punic structures, which, in

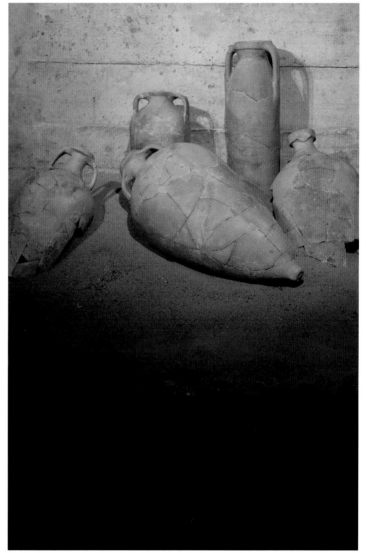

Millennium BCP Archaeological Nucleus
The remains of thousands of years of Lisbon history under the Rua Augusta pavement.

turn, served as a Roman necropolis. This shows signs of both burials and cremation. In a corner of the wall opposite, an 18th-century post-Pombaline drain can be discerned.

The following room contains five salting tanks, lined up on either side, and the Roman pottery used for the preparation and export of the various fish sauces (garum, liquamen, muria and allec). These were, in fact, fermentations of fish remains, fish eggs, seafood, salt and aromatic herbs – highly appreciated by the Roman elite. Here and there are signs of a Pombaline well from the 18th century, part of the Pombaline system of green pine stakes that underpin the buildings in Baixa Pombalina, and even the first drains created for the whole city in that period.

The Roman manufacturing complex, which extends under Rua Augusta, includes a total of 25 tanks and a circular well fed by the groundwater. Slipping through the low corridors, the visitor reaches a small compartment with the remains of a Roman tank belonging to the manufacturing unit, abandoned around the 5th century. A skeleton from the palaeo-Christian period lies there – a trace of a period in which the so-called barbarian peoples divided Iberia among themselves, in 411 AD. Lusitania, including Lisbon, under the name Ulishbona, was dominated by the Alani and then the Germanic tribes of the Visigoths and Suevi, at the beginning of the 5th century.

This area also reveals the base of a Pombaline arch, some foundations and domestic drains from the same period, and a series of Lusitanian amphoras used to contain the fish and seafood preparations exported to almost the whole of Europe.

The final room of the visit presents part of a Roman bathhouse, composed of three pools – the *frigidarium* (cold bath), *caldarium* (hot bath) and *tepidarium* (warm bath) – which surround the first **multicoloured mosaic** *in situ*, dating from the 3rd century AD. It has four panels, decorated in six colours with geometric and intertwining figures in the form of swastikas, squares, peltas, spindles and diamonds.

There are Arab silos situated almost on top of this extraordinary Roman mosaic – a sign of the conquest of Lisbon, Al-Ushbuna, in 714. The occupation lasted until 1147 when King Afonso Henriques took the city, with the help of English, German and Flemish crusaders. A Pombaline kiln for processing iron is also on view, in combination with a forge: its combustion chambers and the lowest ring of its vault, in brick, have been saved in order to demonstrate that Baixa Pombalina was also home to workshops and certain industrial activities in the 14th century, in addition to the ever-present trading. This can still be seen today in some of the Baixa street names, e.g. Rua dos Douradores (gilders), Rua da Prata (silversmiths), Rua do Ouro (goldsmiths), Rua dos Sapateiros (shoemakers), Rua dos Correeiros (sadlers)... On returning to the surface, and the crystal-clear light of Lisbon, it is worth remembering that this Rua da Conceição, now hurriedly crossed to catch Tram 28, also conceals a **Roman Gallery**. It takes the form of a cryptoportico from the time of Augustus (1st c. BC-1st c. AD), a robust vaulted construction, with various galleries and careful masonry consisting of panelled stone arches, a technique typical of the beginning of the Roman Empire. It also contained a pedestal with a Latin inscription, dedicated to Asclepius, the god of medicine, which it is now in the National Museum of Archaeology in Belém. These galleries were discovered during the reconstruction of the city after the 1755 earthquake and still serve as the foundations of Pombaline buildings. In the 19th century, this historic monument, whose dimensions are not known, was used as a cistern by the population of Lisbon. The various circular openings in the crossing point of the vaults are still visible. It was known then as the Rua da Prata Water Reserve and people believed that the water from the well above the Gallery of the Springs – where there is a series of small springs and a crack that extends along the whole length of the floor and the ceiling – had therapeutic effects, hence its name, the Holy-Water Well. Nowadays the crack is monitored by sophisticated equipment.

As the monument is normally below water, it is only open to visitors once a year, generally in August or September, by courtesy of Lisbon City Council. Through a complex logistics operation, it manages to siphon off the water from the area and coordinate entry to the galleries by means of a manhole in the middle of Rua da Conceição. This means controlling the traffic and requires the accompaniment of specialists from the Museum of the City.

But here comes the 28 and it is time to decide on a destination. So let it be Graça, on the east side of the city, by a way that is punctuated with historical landmarks of this timeless Lisbon. The level ground of Rua da Conceição permits a glimpse of the traditional retail trade in the Baixa Pombalina – the old haberdashery and perfume shops, the typical wine and spirit stores, the shops selling international brands, the small cafes...

This is **Lisbon Baixa or Baixa Pombalina**, built by order of the Marquis of Pombal, Secretary of State for War and Foreign Affairs during the reign of King José I, following the 1755 earthquake. It was built with the wealth of the colony of Brazil, where enough gold was found to fill Portugal's coffers for almost two centuries. Covering around 23.5 ha, the area extended from Terreiro do Paço, besides the River Tagus, up to Rossio and Praça da Figueira and, to the sides, from Cais do Sodré, Chiado and Carmo, on the one hand, to the Cathedral and the hill of St George's Castle, on the other.

Lisbon Baixa, as an architectural whole, is based on classical proportions and rules – inspired by the golden ratio. It is an excellent example of a meticulously planned city, with its broad, straight streets, standardised façades, foundations on pine stakes and innovative anti-seismic construction – the Pombaline cage. This consists of a wooden structure covered by masonry walls, with diagonal bracing, also termed St Andrew's Cross format. It sits on a foundation of masonry, with barrel vault arches on the first floor of the building, which allows the energy transmitted by an earthquake to be dispersed without damaging the structure. In addition, all the buildings are separated by masonry firewalls. The reconstruction of Baixa, as a whole, was only completed in 1806.

In its precise geometry, Baixa is formed by a series of straight and perpendicular streets, an architectural design of Eugénio dos Santos and Carlos Mardel, under the supervision of Manuel da Maia. The streets are arranged on either side of a central axis, Rua Augusta, where traditional retailing blends with stores selling international brands and where the very recent **Museum of Design and Fashion (MUDE - Museu do Design e da Moda)** has found its home. It has an important storehouse of hundreds of 20th and 21st-century design and fashion items, from Francisco Capelo's collection.

RUA DA CONCEIÇÃO
Traditional retailing in the Lisbon Baixa (historic centre).

This street has its triumphal arch, a unique landmark in Lisbon – **Rua Augusta Arch (Arco da Rua Augusta)**, erected in homage to King José I. Though it was planned in 1759, construction only began in 1873, on the basis of the architect Veríssimo da Costa's design and the sculptural work of the famous French sculptor Anatole Calmels and his pupil Leandro Braga, who designed the main figures.

The images of Glory crowning Genius and Valour surmount the arch while, below, stand the statues of some of the most illustrious figures of Portuguese history: Viriato, warrior and Lusitanian strategist who fought the Romans from 147-139 BC, the celebrated navigator Vasco da Gama, who discovered the sea route to India in 1498, Nuno Álvares Pereira, the Holy Constable, who affirmed the independence of Portugal from Castile in the famous Battle of Aljubarrota in 1385 and was canonised by Pope Benedict XVI in 2009, and the Marquis of Pombal, who redesigned the city after the 1755 earthquake and is credited with the famous phrase, after the tragedy, "Bury the dead, take care of the living and build the city".

At the side of these historical figures, the allegorical sculptures of Vítor Bastos portray the River Tagus and River Douro, the latter with a bunch of grapes representing the wine growing wealth of the North. On the rear side, there is a large clock, installed in 1941, a time when it had to be regularly wound up and corrected, as the automatic mechanism was only added later.

Inaugurated in 1873, the Arco da Rua Augusta carries a Latin inscription 'Virtutibus maiorum ut sit omnibus documento. P(ecunia). P(ublica). D(icatum)' (To the virtues of our forefathers, as a lesson for all. Raised at public expense), below which it displays the arms of Portugal. At its feet lies Lisbon's most emblematic square and one of the largest in Europe – the historic **Palace Square (Terreiro do Paço) or Commerce Square (Praça do Comércio).**

Here, in sight of the unmistakable blue waters of the River Tagus, visitors can half-close their eyes and imagine the hustle and bustle of people from the four corners of the earth: people from the tropics, European researchers, spies, merchants, ill-clad slaves, beggars, missionaries, ambassadors and VIPs, as they arrived in Lisbon in exotic clothing, speaking strange languages and bringing spices, especially the coveted pepper, and the riches of the East that would revolutionise the habits of 16th-century European courts. At that time, the Terreiro do Paço was the centre of political and economic power and, around it, King Manuel, the all-powerful monarch, created the famous Casa da Mina e da Índia (Mina and India House), where scholars and mapmakers designed the maps of the Discoveries.

Before them, in the 14th century, Lisbon already had an extremely busy seaport. As Fernão Lopes, a chronicler of the time, wrote: "Lisbon is a big city with many hectic people (...) there were Genoese and Placentines and Lombards and Catalans from Aragon and Majorca and Milan, and Corsicans and Biscayans: and other nations, too, to whom the kings gave privileges and liberties".

The hubbub was intense, with over 400 cargo ships right in front of the city, loading wine and salt, and dozens more stretched along the Tagus – also complicating navigation for the small boats that ferried people to either side of the river. The Tagus may be a river but it mingles with the sea, ever-present there, the witness of so much of Lisbon's history – the Tagus, whose sands

MUDE

The original Museum of Design and Fashion (MUDE) in Rua Augusta.

RUA AUGUSTA ARCH

The beautiful arch framing the view towards Terreiro do Paço and the River Tagus.

TERREIRO DO PAÇO
The light at the end of the day in the historic Terreiro do Paço, or Praça do Comércio

have held gold and whose basin, in Roman times, gave Lisbon great wealth, in the form of salt, wine and olive oil, for example.

Dom Dinis, the Poet or Troubadour King (1261-1325) was the first monarch to rule entirely from Lisbon. In his reign, the area that is today the Terreiro do Paço was reclaimed from the sea by draining, new streets such as Rua Nova appeared and Rossio became the centre of Lisbon. The Tagus penetrated the city with inlets that reached as far as Martim Moniz. In Roman times, they served as navigation and river transport channels.

The marble steps on the **Quay of the Columns (Cais das Colunas)** – the two monolithic pillars erected at the end of the 18th century – have been trodden by many illustrious figures of modern times, such as heads of state, including Queen Elizabeth II herself when she visited Lisbon in 1957. During that visit, the President of the Republic, General Craveiro Lopes, is said to have organised grand receptions, with fancy displays, for example, of brigantines – large ships propelled by oars – and period coaches from the magnificent Portuguese collection, newly restored for the occasion.

But there were times when the living wonders of Africa and the East also arrived here, for example, the first elephants seen in Europe since the fall of the Roman Empire. King Manuel I offered one of them, the albino elephant Hanno, to Pope Leo X. Laden with a silver chest full of gold coins, it was part of the luxurious embassy to Rome that Tristão da Cunha led in 1514. It served very well to make the name of the Portuguese monarch famous throughout Europe.

The elephant *Hanno* became the Pope' favourite mascot and, when it died, was buried in the Cortile del Belvedere, with an epitaph composed by the Pontifex himself. It is thought that it was a present from the King of Cochim (Kochi) to Manuel I or was even purchased by the Viceroy of India, Afonso de Albuquerque.

Besides the elephants, this Terreiro do Paço saw the arrival of fierce leopards, jaguars and panthers, coloured parrots, Indian horses and even an incredible rhinoceros, *Ganda*, which was also offered to Pope Leo X in 1517. The creature died, however, when one of the ships was wrecked off Genoa, after calling in at the port of Marseilles to satisfy the curiosity of the King of France, François I. When, later, it was found on the shore, it was stuffed and sent on to the Pope. This fabulous specimen was immortalised by the strokes of the German painter and illustrator Albrecht Dürer (1471-1528). Without even seeing the animal, he drew the famous work of art from reports and a sketch sent from Portugal. This can now be seen in the British Museum in London.

It was here in Terreiro do Paço that King Manuel I wanted to confirm the reports in contemporary treatises on animals that elephants and rhinoceroses were mortal enemies. So he staged a fight between the two animals, proving, in fact, that the rhinoceros scared the mighty elephant. With the curved horn on its snout, the rhinoceros lowered its head and launched itself at the elephant's belly. In fright, the elephant sped off down the ancient streets of the Baixa.

Royal bullfights were also held in this square to entertain the nobility and populace of 17th-century Lisbon. Even before then, historic figures disembarked at the Terreiro do Paço: Philip II, for example, when he arrived in Lisbon after being proclaimed Philip I of Portugal. That was the beginning of the first Philippine dynasty, which would last from 1580 to 1619.

TERREIRO DO PAÇO
The Quay of the Columns (Cais das Colunas) enclosing the waters of the Tagus.

A BAIXA AT NIGHT
The emblematic intersection between Rua da Conceição and Rua Augusta.

To receive Philip III (Philip II of Portugal) in 1619, the Terreiro do Paço was decorated with temporary arches representing various nations and trades. On the Tagus, there were over 300 vessels, some of them quite wonderful – for example, one resembling a carriage riding the waves, prepared to leave: it was drawn by seals and decorated with Tritons and mermaids, with Nepture reigning over all.

In this period of domination by the kings of Spain, the history of the Terreiro do Paço was marked by a violent event, the defenestration of Miguel de Vasconcelos, secretary of state to the Duchess of Mantua, Vicereine of Portugal. Loathed by the Portuguese, he was the first victim of the 1640 Revolution and, in death, the sign that informed the population of the success of the revolt. The conspirators found him hidden in a cupboard in the palace; after riddling his body with gunshot, they threw him out of the window, to the delight of the people.

There were, however, other times when the Terreiro do Paço was decorated for royal celebrations, such as those when Catarina de Bragança left for England, on 20 April 1662, to marry King Charles II. She embarked here at the Terreiro do Paço, with the Tagus full of ships from the British fleet. During those festive days, this important square was taken over by temporary coloured arches, bullfights and music.

Another important royal celebration was staged here for the arrival of the Archduchess of Austria, Maria Ana, daughter of the Holy Roman Emperor. She became Queen of Portugal when she married King João V in 1708. Escorted by a fleet of 18 ships, Maria Ana arrived in Lisbon on 27 October and rode to the court in a convoy of seven magnificent coaches. The public festivities lasted three days, with the construction of an amphitheatre for bullfights and with a simulation of Mount Etna erupting, in the middle of Terreiro do Paço.

It was Lisbon's golden age, as the port of the world and the deluxe market for European elites. Merchants from the whole of Europe settled in Lisbon, mixing with Jews, Muslims, African slaves, Indians, Chinese and Japanese people, and even native peoples from Brazil. Gold from Guinea and the Gold Coast, silk from China and India, every kind of oriental spice (cloves, nutmeg, cinnamon and malagueta peppers), cane sugar and musk were some of the treasures marketed in the capital. The huge trading profits were used to construct important buildings such as Jeronimos Monastery, the Tower of Belém (thus inaugurating the new Manueline style), and the palace in Terreiro do Paço.

But this vibrant and prosperous scene would also be marked by *autos-de-fé* (acts of faith – the burning of heretics at the stake) in Terreiro do Paço in the 18th century. The first *auto-de-fé* had taken place in Rossio in 1540. It was the age of conflict between the elite descended from the old aristocracy and the new social class of the "New Christians" (forced converts), who were also in ascent in the reign of King Manuel I. This was also the period when the Inquisition was installing itself in the Iberian Peninsula and – in 1569 – the great plague ravaged Lisbon.

The square still contains part of the palaces where the kings of Portugal resided over a period of two centuries, after King Manuel I transferred his residence from Castelo S. Jorge to this magnificent site beside the river. The first palace was destroyed in the terrible earthquake of 1755, along with the whole 70,000-volume library and the archive holding the most important documents on Portuguese seafaring and seafarers. With a magnitude of 9 on the Richter scale, the quake struck on the morning of 1 November 1755, All Saints Day, shaking the city with tremendous force. This was followed by fires that burned for almost 5 days and, two hours after the shock itself, a tsunami that submerged the port and city centre.

The Lisbon Baixa of the 18th century – rich and noble, despite the dirt and urban disarray, and endowed with countless churches and convents – evaporated in an enormous cloud of dust. At the time, the city had 150,000-200,000 inhabitants, many of whom were in church as it was a religious holiday. They rushed to the banks of the Tagus in the hope of catching a boat to the other side, but the giant wave swept through the city as far as the present-day Praça do Rossio. It is presumed that, in all, around 30,000 people lost their lives in Lisbon's greatest tragedy ever, a tragedy that would echo throughout Europe and become the first truly global event.

This episode was to create a confrontation between the two contemporary visions of the world in Europe – a dogmatic and conservative vision, based on religion, according to which everything was governed by the divine will, and the theories of the Enlightenment, which were already revealing the beginnings of the scientific movement and an attempt to understand the laws of nature.

Like other European philosophers, Voltaire reflected on the catastrophe, even to the point of writing his 'Poem on the Lisbon Disaster' – "Did Lisbon, which is no longer, have more vices/ than London or Paris, which are drowning in pleasure?/ Lisbon in ruins, dancing in Paris." He wrote another literary work, 'Candide or Optimism', a philosophical narrative that takes a critical view of the tragic event and the related conservative ideas. Struck by the magnitude of the Lisbon earthquake, Immanuel Kant ultimately wrote three texts on the subject, after collecting all the information available at the time. According to his theory, which attempted to explain that the phenomenon had a natural cause, there were enormous underground caverns full of hot gases: by shifting, they caused the earthquake.

The question put the spotlight on a series of philosophical and practical issues. The Marquis of Pombal himself ordered a survey of every parish in the country to ascertain the facts regarding the occurrence and the effects of the earthquake, in the first attempt to describe a natural phenomenon objectively. The data from this survey, considered the precursor of seismology, is stored in the Torre do Tombo. Lying next to a tectonic fault line, Lisbon had already suffered other less important quakes before 1755 but, even now, the geological causes of the seismic activity in the region are a question of scientific debate.

The fact is that, after the 1755 earthquake, the Terreiro do Paço was no longer the site of a royal residence. King José I was so terrified by the episode that he never returned to Lisbon and never took up residence again in a stone palace: he lived in the Barraca Real (Royal Hut) erected in Ajuda. The monument in the middle of the Terreiro do Paço, the bronze equestrian statue, was erected in his honour – it was the first of its kind to be cast in Portugal and is the oldest public statue in Lisbon. It stands on a pedestal of Pêro Pinheiro lias stone, flanked by allegorical statues of Triumph and Renown, with a large shield in front displaying the royal coat of arms, along with a medallion portraying the Marquis of Pombal. The rear side contains an allegory in low relief, alluding to the king's generosity in his efforts to rebuild the city. It is worth mentioning the snakes under the horses' hooves, symbolising evil. A curious piece of information is that pigeons have never landed on the statue.

The nobility also moved further away from the centre of the capital, to areas such as Ajuda and Lapa. The buildings erected here in the meantime in the reconstruction of the city were first occupied by the Lisbon Stock Exchange, though they have been used since by official bodies – e.g. the Ministries of Finance, Home Affairs and Justice and the Supreme Court. Under the arches, only a single reference point of the city's poetry and culture remains – the historic Café-Restaurant Martinho da Arcada, established in 1782. This site has maintained, intact, the table where one of the greatest Portuguese poets used to write, Fernando Pessoa (1888-1935), a figure famous for writings in which he divided himself among various personalities, known as heteronymns.

The Terreiro do Paço was also the stage for illustrious visits in the first years of the 20th century, during the reign of Carlos I, the last King of Portugal. For example, Edward VII of the United Kingdom was received here, as were the president of the French Republic, Émile Loubet, and, later, Queen Alexander of the United Kingdom, in the company of Princesses Maud and Victoria.

But another tragedy would take place in this Terreiro do Paço on 1 February 1908. After disembarkation from the steamboat bringing the Royal Family to Lisbon at the end of the season in the Ducal Palace of Vila Viçosa, King Carlos I and his son Luís Filipe were assassinated as their carriage crossed the square. The assassins were killed on the spot by the royal guard and later identified as members of the republican movement, who first revolted in Oporto on 31 January 1891. The royal tombs are located in the House of Bragança Mausoleum (Panteão dos Reis da Dinastia de Bragança at Mosteiro de São Vicente de Fora), which lies close to one of the Tram 28 stops on the way to Graça.

In 1918, a procession took place in the Terreiro do Paço to salute the heads of state and foreign delegations for the Allied victory in the First World War. On 25 April 1974, another political event occurred here when the square was taken over by tanks, officers and the population in the revolt by the Armed Forces Movement, led by Captain Salgueiro Maia. This brought down the government of Marcello Caetano and the Estado Novo, in a revolution that became famous the world over for its symbol – a red carnation.

On 12 May 2010 a crowd estimated at 80,000 people attended the mass celebrated by Pope Benedict XVI in the Terreiro do Paço. The fine altar was particularly noteworthy – a platform measuring 39 m by 12 m, covered by a partly transparent canopy that allowed a glimpse of the Tagus, dotted with over a hundred vessels.

But Tram 28 now heads for its first slope, in Rua da Conceição. The pavements of translucent stone are gleaming – the famous Portuguese mosaic made up of white limestone and black basalt cubes. This luxurious taste had its beginnings in the 16th century, when Portuguese trade with the world brought great wealth.

The present-day **Church of Mary Magdalene (Igreja da Madalena)** now appears in sight, the result of various reconstructions of the original church, which was built there in 1150 or 1164 by order of King Afonso Henriques. It stood next to the Moorish

ENGRAVED STONES FROM ROMAN TIMES
Roman remains built into a side wall in Travessa do Almada.

CHURCH OF MARY MAGDALENE (IGREJA DA MADALENA)
The fine stone carving in the façade of the church, rebuilt by Queen Maria I.

wall, the Arab fortifications raised by the Muslims between the middle of the 10th century and 1147, when Afonso Henriques conquered Lisbon.

After a fire in 1363, King Fernando I had the church rebuilt but in 1600 it was partly destroyed by a cyclone and in 1755 it collapsed in the earthquake. In 1783, Queen Maria I had the church rebuilt from the foundations and, fifty years later, it was also altered. The Manueline portico, with a trilobate arch surmounted by two armillary spheres, may have belonged to another church, Nossa Senhora da Conceição dos Freires. This was also destroyed in the earthquake.

Near this church, there are **four engraved stones from Roman times**, built into the side wall of a building in Travessa do Almada. They are also called the Pedras Negras Stones (Lápides das Pedras Negras) as they were discovered near the street of that name. One of them is an offering to the goddess Cybele and, according to the expert in Lisbon history, Augusto Vieira da Silva (1896-1951), it was found with the other three stones in a cluster of Roman remains, possibly even the ruins of the temple of the goddess. The remains were discovered in 1753 and 1754 when building work began on the site.

One more bend and Tram 28 reaches the Square, **Church and Museum of St Anthony (Largo, Igreja and Museu de Santo António)** – the unofficial patron saint of Lisbon. His feast day is on 13 June, when Lisbon City Hall also sponsors a collective wedding ceremony, given that he is considered the matchmaker saint. In the square, the visitor will find a statue to him, cast in bronze and signed by Soares Branco. Another custom maintained by the church and the faithful on his day is to distribute bread rolls among the poor, the famous "St Anthony's rolls", which are kept in a food tin so that there is no shortage of food throughout the year.

Lisbon's most popular church stands on the site of the house where St Anthony is said to have been born in 1195. The crypt, which can be entered via the sacristy, is all that remains of the original mediaeval church, another building destroyed in the earthquake. The Church of St Anthony of Lisbon was only built between 1757 and 1787, to the designs of Mateus Vicente de Oliveira, the architect of the Basilica of Estrela, which Tram 28 also passes on its way to Prazeres.

The exterior combines a João V-style Baroque portal, a Rococo commemorative plaque on the southern façade and Neoclassical Ionic columns flanking the main entrance. Consisting of an aisle-less nave, the Church of St Anthony is covered with a barrel-vault ceiling and decorated with a large amount of marble. It was partly paid for with the alms collected by children who begged for "a coin for St Anthony" in the streets of Lisbon.

The beauty of Pedro Alexandrino's paintings in the chapel, the mid-to-late 18th-century tiled panel in the sacristy, and the architect Vasco Regaleira's neo-mediaeval railings, imitating the famous railings of Lisbon Cathedral, show the importance of this national monument. On the way to the crypt, there is another tiled panel, this time modern, commemorating Pope John Paul II's visit in 1982. A theologian and an outstanding preacher, St Anthony was an Augustinian monk in Coimbra in 1210 and a conventual Franciscan father in 1220. He travelled to Italy and France where he delivered innumerable dissertations to Franciscans and Dominicans alike. He also managed to attend the canonisation

ST ANTHONY'S CHURCH (IGREJA DE SANTO ANTÓNIO)
Statue of the matchmaker saint, unofficial patron saint of Lisbon.

of St Francis in 1228. He died in October 1231 and, today, his mortal remains lie in the basilica to his memory in Padua, Italy.

So, crowded with tourists and city residents, Tram 28 speeds on up the hill towards **Lisbon Cathedral (Sé de Lisboa)**, the oldest monument in the city – classified as part of the national heritage since 1907. The driver rings the bell and the "ping-ping"echoes beyond the hill. Straight ahead, the stone façade of the centuries-old cathedral marks one of Lisbon's most historic settings.

Started only three years after the city was taken from the Moors in 1147, Lisbon Cathedral was built on the site of the former Almoravid mosque and presented to the first bishop of Lisbon, the English crusader Gilbert Hastings. Originally called the Church of St Mary the Great, it was devastated by three earthquakes in the 15th century and again by the one in 1755, which meant that over the centuries it has undergone a constant process of renewal. The original design and the first parts to be built were traced out between 1150 and the first years of the 13th century. The design adopted was identical to that of Coimbra Cathedral, with two aisles, a triforium (gallery) above the aisles, a projecting transept and a high altar with three parts.

Robust and massive in scale, the cathedral recalls the military and defensive characteristics of its time. Romanesque and Gothic in style, it was designed by the master-builder Roberto, a famous French-born architect of the 12th century, who was also mainly responsible for Coimbra Cathedral. Its façade, with the sundial, the two battlemented bell towers and the **exquisite rose window**, gives it that characteristically Romanesque appearance.

The building consists of a nave and two aisles with six ceiling sections, two apses flanking a simple chancel, and solid walls interrupted by narrow openings that allow in a little light. There is also the high triforium – the narrow open gallery above the arches – which was reconstructed with Romanesque arches running the length of the nave.

In subsequent centuries, the cathedral underwent a series of transformations, in particular with the construction of the Chapel of Bartolomeu Joanes, on the north side of the main entrance. It contains the tomb of this rich Lisbon merchant and high official at the court of King Dinis (14th c.). It is worth noting the Portuguese Gothic cloister of the same period and the new, distinctly Gothic altar in the ambulatory, which King Afonso IV had built as his family mausoleum. The 1755 earthquake had a serious impact on the building, destroying part of the cloister, the chancel and the transept tower. King José I reconstructed the chancel. Later renovation added Neoclassical decoration, which almost masked the Romanesque and Gothic styles. But the restoration efforts at the beginning of the 20th century reinstated these architectural styles, transforming **Lisbon Cathedral into the only Romanesque and Gothic building in the capital**.

Visitors enter the cathedral via a deep porch and a doorway framed by four archivolts on small smooth columns with elongated shafts, surmounted by eight capitals displaying figurative and plant decoration.

The interior of the cathedral is dark and appears bare, with almost nothing remaining of the decoration carried out by King João V in the first half of the 18th century. The new sacristy was built in 1649 by the architect Marcos de Magalhães, with the particularity that the statuary only portrayed Portuguese saints. The marble inlay work and a large and attractive chest complete the decoration.

Reconstructed after the 1755 earthquake, the chancel is different from the rest of the building, as its style is Baroque. However, the date of construction and the architect are not exactly known.

The Chapel of St Ildefonso contains the **impressive 14th-century carved stone sarcophagi** of Lopo Fernandes Pacheco, King Afonso IV's comrade-in-arms, and his wife, who has a book of hours in her hands and dogs at her feet. Also still standing is an intricate mediaeval cast-iron railing, probably from the 13th century, which must have belonged to the original Romanesque cathedral design and been re-worked for this chapel. A side chapel holds the new tombs of King Afonso IV and his wife, Queen Beatriz, as the original ones were lost in the 1755 earthquake.

In this semicircle around the chancel – the famous ambulatory or *charola*, with its nine pointed-arch chapels, typical of the great mediaeval pilgrim churches – there are other historical and surprising radial or apsidal chapels, such as the Franciscan chapel with the font where St Anthony was baptised in 1195. This also contains tiled panels representing the saint preaching to the fish. It recalls the famous 'St Anthony's Sermon to the Fish', a Portuguese Baroque literary work penned by Father António Vieira, a great Jesuit writer and orator, who was also baptised in Lisbon Cathedral. He died in Brazil in 1697 after defending the abolition of slavery and miraculously escaping the sentence of death handed down by the Inquisition.

It is worth noting the chapel with a **Baroque nativity scene by Machado de Castro, sculpted out of cork** (one of Portugal's most characteristic materials), wood and terracotta or, again, the chapel of the unknown princess, with its 14th-century reclining statue. There are other Gothic tombs and sarcophagi spread through the eastern gallery, including the tombs in the Misericórdia Chapel, with the reclining statues of Dona Margarida Abernaz and an unknown bishop.

The Bartolomeu Joanes Chapel is also worth seeing, with its eight-panel altarpiece representing the martyrdom of St Bartholomew. It was commissioned in 1537 by the humanist Pedro Fernandes de Serpa. In addition, there are various scenes from the life of the Virgin and the Passion of Christ, painted by noteworthy Portuguese painters such as Cristóvão de Figueiredo, Garcia Fernandes and Diogo Contreiras.

The very fine Gothic cloister, from somewhere around 1300, i.e. the reign of King Dinis, has elegant double arches and beautiful sculptured stone capitals. This contrasts with the archaeological work in progress, which allows a glimpse of archaeological remains from the early Iron Age, Phoenician remains (6th-5th c. BC orientalising pottery) and vestiges of 1st c. AD Roman occupation (paving with a drain and two walls) and Arab occupation (domestic pottery and food remains such as animal bones and fish scales).

In the south wing of the cloister there is a building that, with some probability, may have been part of the great mosque, which was demolished when the cathedral was built. Its walls still contain horizontal stripes painted in red and white and a vaulted recess.

The **cathedral treasure** can be found at the top of the staircase immediately to the right of the main entrance. It has a very extensive collection of silver, church vestments, statuary, illuminated manuscripts, and relics associated with St Vincent – the patron saint of Lisbon – including one item that is particularly precious: the mother of pearl chest with the saint's presumed mortal remains, which were brought to Lisbon from Cabo de São Vicente in 1173.

LISBON CATHEDRAL (SÉ DE LISBOA)
The sundial showing the time on one of the Cathedral façades and another rose window around the corner.

The play of light and shade on the stone beauty of the Cathedral.

LISBON CATHEDRAL (SÉ DE LISBOA)
A moment of sunshine on the deep porch of the city's oldest monument.

PUBLIC CONVENIENCES BESIDE THE CATHEDRAL (CASA DE BANHO PÚBLICA JUNTO À SÉ)
The ruined façade of a pre-earthquake residence in Lisbon (i.e. pre-1755).

According to legend, two sacred crows escorted the boat carrying the remains of the saint, who was martyred in Valencia, Spain. Both the crows and the boat – which arrived at Cabo de São Vicente in the Algarve – became emblems of the city of Lisbon and it is said that the descendants of these original crows used to live in the cathedral cloister.

One of the most valuable objects in the chapter house is **the famous 1760 Monstrance**, a splendid example of the goldsmith's art, by Joaquim Caetano de Carvalho. Though commissioned by King João V in 1748, it was presented by King José I. Wrought in solid gold and decorated with 4120 precious stones, the monstrance is 94 cm in height and weighs over 17 kg. It is also worth noting the set of patriarchal items, made up of the gestatorial chair, flabella (fans) and tiara, work from 18th-century Italy.

The defenestration of the Bishop of Lisbon, Dom Martinho, a Castilian, marked a truly tragic event in the history of the venerable Cathedral of Lisbon. On the night of 6 December 1383, he was dining with his guests when they noticed a great disturbance in front of the church. In a state of excitation, the population of Lisbon believed that the Mestre de Avis (Master of Avis), the future King João I, had indeed murdered the Count of Ourém, João Fernandes Andeiro, the lover and ally of Dona Leonor Teles. This noblewoman was opposed to the Mestre de Avis and preferred a Castilian victory in the crisis over the succession to the Portuguese throne in the wake of King Fernando's death.

It was a delicate situation because the people demanded that the cathedral bells be rung to announce the good news, but the bishop hesitated, uncertain of what was happening. Distrusting the bishop's attitude, in addition to the fact that he was Castilian, the people attacked the cathedral and some of their representatives climbed the tower to confront the bishop. But then they hesitated to kill him, as they were convinced of his innocence, which led the angry crowd to think that they were all colluding in favour of the Castilian party.

To save their own skins, the people's representatives threw the bishop out the window, along with his guests, who were no lesser dignitaries than the Prior of Guimarães and a notary from Silves. The poor bishop's lifeless body was then dragged through the streets to Rossio.

Finally, right there beside the cathedral, in the **public conveniences next to the Tram 28 stop (casa de banho pública)**, the history of pre-earthquake Lisbon can be seen at the bottom of the narrow steps beyond the dark-green iron gate. In this area, which was levelled during the reconstruction of the city after the 1755 earthquake, traces of the residential quarter that existed there can still be seen – part of the entry to a house, with a large doorway and ashlar door posts, in addition to a window and round pebble paving.

Maria Alexandra Borda D'Água Carvalho Marques, the caretaker, was kind enough to photocopy a text with the details of this archaeological find, which was discovered in 1993 during the building work for the public conveniences. "I found this text during some tidying up at the Cathedral Parish Council Offices and instantly thought of having it at hand to give the tourists who come here", she said with a smile, as the guardian of this little bit of the city's history, almost concealed there. The toilets, impeccable by the way, are open 9 am-12 noon and 2-6 pm from Monday to Saturday.

II. The road to Graça

Above Lisbon Cathedral, a sober building on the left at the next bend deserves mention – **Aljube Prison (Prisão do Aljube)**, rebuilt over an older one, which also served as a prison for the Inquisition in 1536, a prison for criminals condemned to the galleys, perhaps the residence of the Archbishop of Lisbon, Miguel de Castro, whose coat of arms are above the doorway (dated between 1568 and 1652), and even a women's prison in the 19th century. The name Aljube comes from the Arabic word "aljubb", meaning "well".

In 1930 this prison began to receive the political prisoners of the Estado Novo (dictatorship) for interrogation – well-known figures such as Miguel Torga, one of the most important 20th century Portuguese writers, and Hermínio da Palma Inácio, a mythical figure in the anti-Salazar resistance and the only prisoner to escape from there, in an act of extreme daring. Even the ex-President of the Republic, Mário Soares. As a child, he came to visit his father, another opponent of the Salazar regime, and, as a young militant in the MUDJ (the youth wing of the Democratic Unity Movement), which opposed the Salazar regime, he was held here in 1948.

The building was closed after the April 25 Revolution but, in the meantime, has been occupied by the headquarters of the Social Reintegration Institute. A tablet attached to the façade bears witness to the struggle for freedom that took place there too, with the resistance of the political prisoners. It bears the words: "Here, from the silence of the 'drawers', of a motherland that was gagged, of the breasts that were broken by the torture of the PIDE [political police], rose the cry for freedom, from here April blossomed."

But right at the side of this building, with its harrowing memory, a stairway leads to another time in the history of Lisbon – the **Roman Theatre Museum (Museu do Teatro Romano)**. Housed in part of an 18th-century building, the former stables of the

Lisbon Cathedral Chapter, the museum is divided into various areas, including an exhibition room with different finds from the various archaeological excavations since 1967, an archaeological site, and a fine patio garden with a view of the Tagus. Behind the museum, across Rua de São Mamede, lie the ruins of the Roman theatre itself.

The Roman theatre in Lisbon was built under Augustus, at the beginning of the Empire (1st c. AD) and remodelled under Nero in 57 AD. The sole example of its kind in Portuguese territory, it was built to hold an audience of 3000-5000 people. After being abandoned in the fourth century AD, it remained buried until 1798, when the ruins were discovered during the reconstruction of the city after the 1755 earthquake. Under the zinc roofing it is possible to see part of the stone benches, the seating arrangements, the stage and the *proscenium* arch, along with the holes in the ground where posts were placed to support the stage backdrop.

The exhibition in the room at the museum entrance presents a series of items recovered during excavations, such as the fine white marble statue of 'Silenus Sleeping' (1st c. AD), Ionic and Corinthian capitals, column shafts, parts of the *proscenium* wall in grey and reddish marble, with part of the dedication to Nero, and a fragment of a white marble low relief portraying the Muse of Tragedy. Other precious items include Roman coins from different periods, from the Emperor Trajan (98-117 AD) to Theodosius (393-395 AD).

The archaeological site, which is visible from the first floor of the museum, contains 17th and 18th-century housing structures, built against the retaining wall of the theatre. There are also large olive oil pots and amphoras lying around the small terrace and the viewing terrace. On the walls of the theatre, there are also traces of later buildings, such as silos from Islamic times and the remains of mediaeval houses.

Tram 28 now hurries its way to Graça but it first has to make regular stops in this street, which changes its name every few dozen metres – Rua Augusto Rosa, beside the Cathedral, Largo de São Martinho, a tiny corner of the road, and Rua do Limoeiro, where nature makes its mark with a **curious example of a leafy Filotaica Dioica**. It is said that this tree, with its protuberant roots in the air, is almost 300 years old.

But behind the balmy shade that the tree casts over the pavement lie the walls of another prison that was still operating in the 20th century – the **Limoeiro Prison (Prisão de Limoeiro)**. In 1771 it held the dauntless poet, Bocage, Portuguese literature's greatest proponent of Arcadism (the literary school whose main feature was the glorification of nature) and the author of famous satires and erotic poetry. However, the history of the place is even more complicated, as this was the Paço dos Infantes, the home of the children of the Prince Pedro and his beloved Inês de Castro. This couple's legendary love for each other turned to tragedy, with the execution of Inês and her posthumous acclamation as queen.

This site has also been known as the Palace of the Mint (Paço das Moedas), as coins were minted here, and Palace-near-St Martin's (Paço de A-Par-de S. Martinho), as there was a nearby church dedicated to the saint. It was connected to the royal palace by an arch. Finally, it has also been known as the Lemon Tree Palace (Paço do Limoeiro).

King Fernando and Queen Leonor Teles, who married in secret, lived here. The queen would play an important role in the conflict that occurred from 1383-1385 between the Master of Avis, the

THE ROMAN THEATRE MUSEUM (MUSEU DO TEATRO ROMANO)
The ruins of the only Roman theatre in Portugal from the first century AD.

THE ROAD TO GRAÇA
Tram 28 rolls along apace on one of the city's hills.

**VIEWING TERRACE OF ST LUZIA
(MIRADOURO DE SANTA LUZIA)**
Another glance over the blue Tagus.

future King João, and the King of Castile, Philip I. It was right here that the Master of Avis stabbed the Count of Ourém, the friend of the queen and representative of the Spanish party in the crisis over the succession to the Portuguese throne. This provoked the death of the Bishop of Lisbon, who was thrown from the window in the tower of Lisbon Cathedral (as explained in Chapter I). Nowadays, this site is used by the Centre for Legal Studies.

Meanwhile, the route of 28 is about to arrive at the first of the viewing terraces (miradouros) on this hill – the **Belvedere of St Luzia (Miradouro de Santa Luzia)**, an area open to the river, with its garden and mirror of water, tile panel, bust of the historian Júlio de Castilho, and pergola hanging over the blue of the Tagus. In the springtime, vivid bougainvilleas – dark carmine, almost violet – come into flower. At this tram stop, the voice of the driver can be heard announcing – *Castle, Château, Castillo* – and, in fact, the notice in front indicates the way to **St George's Castle (Castelo de São Jorge)**. The castle was classified as a national monument in 1910. It has had a long and turbulent history since it was built around the 10th and 11th centuries, a time when Lisbon, or Al-Ushbuna, was an important Muslim port city. Situated on one of the highest hills in Lisbon, the Castelo de São Jorge has been occupied by humans since the Iron Age (6th c. BC). In the first century BC, the great Greek geographer and philosopher Strabo mentioned that Olisipo had been fortified in the second century BC during the Roman military campaigns in what was then Lusitania.

But it was under the Arabs that the castle and its strong walls, which defended the casbah, appeared in the geography of the city and the reports of Arab geographers. The fortress was the centre of political and military power, serving simultaneously as the residence of the governing class, nobles and senior public servants. King Afonso Henriques conquered Lisbon in 1147 – after a three-month siege, with the support of Norman, Flemish, German and English Crusaders who were on the way to the Holy Land. The castle then became a royal residence, when the first Portuguese monarch was in the city, and continued to fulfil this role from the time that Lisbon became the capital of the kingdom in 1256 until the beginning of the 16th century. It was also the bishop's palace and the residence of noble families at court.

After the wars with Castile at the end of the 14th century, King João I placed the castle under the protection of St George, the patron saint of warriors and the Christian faith. In the Royal Palace in the Fortress (Paço Real da Alcáçova), the famous navigator Vasco da Gama was received by King Manuel I when he returned from India in 1498. And to mark the birth of the future King João III, the first Portuguese theatre play was presented here – *Monólogo do Vaqueiro* (The Cowboy's Soliloquy) by Gil Vicente, one of the greatest names in Portuguese literature and playwriting.

When the royal family and the court moved to Terreiro do Paço, where the new Riverside Palace (Paço da Ribeira) had meanwhile been built, in the 16th century, Castelo de São Jorge lost its importance. It was only in the middle of that century that another king resided there, King Sebastian, the only son of Prince John and grandson of King John III. The young king's death in the famous battle of Alcácer-Quibir in 1578 gave rise both to the legend that, on a foggy day, he would return and give succour to Portugal and to a secular and mystical movement in the country. This even reached Brazil at the end of the 19th century, in the War of Canudos, a struggle between the tillers of the land and the Republic of Brazil.

ST GEORGE'S CASTLE (CASTELO DE SÃO JORGE)

The profile of the former Moorish Castle dominates the city.

Sebastian was the last king to live in the old palace in the castle. On his death, the crown of Portugal passed to King Philip I of Portugal, Philip II of Spain. In 1581, he had a body – allegedly that of the late king – transferred to the Jeronimos Monastery (Mosteiro dos Jerónimos). The marble tomb, resting on two elephants, can still be seen but the doubts about its authenticity have persisted for over 425 years.

Under the "Philippine" domination of Portugal, the castle regained military importance. It was adapted and improved to serve the Spanish garrison and even became a prison, a role that it retained until the 1940s. In the 1755 earthquake, large parts of the castle were lost, including various buildings, towers and sections of the walls. It was only (partly) reconstructed in 1910, when it was classified as a national monument. In 1940, to commemorate the Birth of the Nation and the Restoration of Independence, work was carried out that practically re-erected the buildings and walls in accordance with a notion of the most emblematic elements of the castle in its various periods of existence.

So what the visitor sees today is a construction that was idealised to represent the Portuguese nation. There are only a few original traces of the thousand-year-old castle, in particular the Fortress (Alcáçova) and some of the rooms in the Old Royal Palace (Antigo Paço Real) such as the Pointed Arch Room, Room of the Columns and Room of the Cisterns (Sala Ogival, Sala das Colunas and Sala das Cisternas), in addition to the eight towers and the four gateways (portas) allowing entry – Porta de São Jorge, Porta de Santa Maria da Alcáçova, Porta do Martim Moniz and Porta Norte.

According to 15th century reports, the room that now contains the restaurant "Casa do Leão" (Lion House) was a wing that housed "two very strong lions, the most beautiful we have ever seen", in the words of Jerónimo Münzer, the German traveller who wrote a log of a journey to Lisbon in the years 1494-95, at the end of the reign of King John II (1455-1495). The Castelejo, the part of the castle on the top of the hill in the area most difficult to reach, is still standing. It is 50 m wide and has 11 towers, including the keep (Torre de Menagem), the strongest and most important tower and the command centre in an attack, and the Ulysses Tower (Torre de Ulisses), the former Record Office of the Kingdom, where the Royal Archives were kept.

There is a wonderful view of Lisbon from Praça de Armas, in the upper part of Castelo de São Jorge or, as it has also been called, Castelo dos Mouros (Castle of the Moors). In the late afternoon, when the light of the sun spills over the slopes of the castle hill and the roofs of Alfama and scintillates in the blue waters of the Tagus, the city almost floats, suspended in the celestial blue of the sky.

But it is time to return to the Miradouro de Santa Luzia to see another church, the **Church of St Luzia (Igreja de Santa Luzia)**, not because it is an imposing building but because it displays the Maltese Cross on the pediment of its simple façade. The original church was built during the reign of King Afonso Henriques, the first King of Portugal, in the 12th century, with the help of the Knights of the Order of Malta. Their tombs can be found inside the church, along with two painted tile panels representing Praça do Comércio and the capture of Lisbon from the Moors. The present-day edifice, which was also built on top of the Moorish Walls, dates from the 18th century, after the 1755 earthquake.

The 28 tram route goes on round the next curve to reveal the beauty of the **Square of the Gates of the Sun (Largo das Portas do**

CHURCH OF ST LUCY
(IGREJA DE SANTA LUZIA)
The church of the Knights of the Order of Malta.

page 53:
SQUARE OF THE GATES OF THE SUN
(LARGO DAS PORTAS DO SOL)
The beauty of the Tagus, again.

Sol), with its magnificent view over the Lisbon's eastern quarters and the River Tagus. Broad and peaceful at that point, it calls for contemplation from this incredible public veranda over the city. From this viewing terrace, with a vista stretching out in the form of a natural amphitheatre, some of the most iconic monuments on Lisbon's skyline can be seen. These include the proud and imposing Church of St Vicente de Fora, the bright dome of the National Mausoleum, the Churches of Michael and St Stephen, and the whole of the distinctive neighbourhood of Alfama. It spreads out below the visitor's gaze, with its maze of streets and lanes, patios, little squares, and twisting stone stairways leading to the banks of the Tagus.

Known in Arabic as Baba al-Maqbara, this square owes its name to one of the gates in the Old or Moorish Walls, the one that faced east, towards the light of the morning sun. In the Islamic period, this entry to the Medina bore that name, Baba al-Maqbara, or Gate of the Almocávar, the old Muslim cemetery situated on the slopes of St Vicente de Fora. In fact, a statue of the martyr St Vincent, patron saint of the city, stands there as if guarding the magnificent view from this *miradouro*.

Parts of the eastern stretch of the **Old Wall (Cerca Velha)**, now a national monument, may be seen here near the Largo das Portas do Sol, in particular some of the stone-coloured towers. One of them, on the other side of the road, almost in the middle of the reddish façade of the Azurara Palace, is almost intact. The palace serves today as the headquarters of the Ricardo do Espírito Santo Foundation, which possesses a notable collection of Portuguese decorative art.

Near the steps leading down to the narrow streets of Alfama, there is another part of this incredible defensive wall, most probably built in the late Roman period (3rd-5th centuries) and used and strengthened during the Islamic occupation of Lisbon (8th-12th centuries).

Close observation of the stones that make up this part of the wall reveals the different types of block used there – e.g. panelled Roman blocks – and the different levels of the wall, which has been steadily rebuilt and repaired over the centuries since its original construction, including in Roman times.

This wall protected the Muslim city, enclosing an area of over 15 hectares. It must have been more than 1250 metres long and 2-2.5 metres thick. When Al-Ushbuna was at its zenith, this area almost doubled in size, including two other adjacent areas, and, at the end of the 11th century, the city had 20,000-30,000 inhabitants. This put it on an equal footing with other great ports in the Iberian Peninsular, e.g. Malaga and Almeria (in present-day Spain).

The main point of architectural interest in this Largo das Portas do Sol is the very fine **Palácio Azurara**, with its red-coloured façade, its noble doorway in 17th-century Classical style, its decorative pediment and floral design, its pilasters, and its windows with pale ashlar masonry. It was built in the 17th century but the date and author of the original plan are not known for certain. The palace may have incorporated certain buildings that were set into the Moorish Wall between the two towers, as there is evidence of their existence on the site in 1573.

Since 1947, Palácio Azurara has been an 18th-century aristocratic house. It was transformed by the hand of the banker, arts patron, collector and "Renaissance prince", Ricardo do Espírito Santo Silva, who decorated it with pieces from his private collection and began an unprecedented cultural project in the capital.

**THE MOORISH WALLS
(CERCA MOURA)**

*Between the Tagus and the stones
of the old walls (Cerca Velha).*

This important collection of Portuguese decorative art was donated to the Portuguese state in 1953, giving rise to the **Ricardo do Espírito Santo Silva Foundation**. This includes an extremely well-endowed museum, a tertiary-level School of Decorative Arts, an Institute of Arts and Crafts, 18 workshops (specialising in the most traditional manufacturing techniques, from the arts of woodwork and metalwork to bookbinding and book decoration, decorative painting, gilding, upholstery and textiles), and a conservation and restoration laboratory.

The Museum and School of Portuguese Decorative Arts is, then, a veritable jewel reflecting the refined atmosphere of 18th-century Portugal. High-quality artistic pieces dating from the 15th to the 18th centuries are arranged in a sophisticated manner, in a singular exhibition that encompasses furniture, textiles, gold and silver work, porcelain, faïence, painted tiles and painting.

The most important part of the collection is, undoubtedly, the furniture. The rooms on the various floors of the museum have extraordinary works of art on show, for example, a **16th-century Namban oratorio**, a splendid cutlery case from the period 1720-1750, a very fine 17th-century bureau with inlaid motifs in precious woods, an 18th-century multi-purpose table, and another series of furniture items in the styles of King José and Queen Maria I, which are representative of the taste of the times.

The textile section includes tapestries (in particular a very rare 16th-century Franco-Flemish tapestry, **Triumphal Procession with Giraffes**), Arraiolos carpets, and embroidered bedspreads and fabrics reflecting Eastern influences – and characterising the originality of 17th and 18th-century Portuguese art. The exhibition also contains an important set of secular Portuguese silverware from the 15th to the 19th centuries and a large quantity of Chinese export porcelain.

Part of the *in situ* collection of painted tiles already belonged to the palace, while others were installed during the restoration work. In addition, there are examples of 18th-century Portuguese faïence, mainly from the famous Real Fábrica do Rato. In the painting section, the notable and rare collection contains 16th-18th century works by important Portuguese and resident foreign artists.

The range of artworks is completed with the collections of drawings and engravings, sculptures, books, documents and bookbindings, iluminated manuscripts and timepieces. At the entrance to the museum there is an exceptional coach, a Berlin-Coupé from 1760-1770 and, through the side door, the Ricardo do Espírito Santo Silva Foundation has installed a shop. It displays pieces produced in the Foundation's furniture and decorative art workshops. On leaving this beautiful Largo das Portas do Sol, Tram 28 penetrates **one of the most picturesque parts of the route to Graça** – extremely narrow lanes, from which it eventually emerges in front of the impressive church and monastery of St Vicente de Fora. With the jerks and jolts of the first tight bend, which marks a new descent along the route, the 28 moves into the **Escolas Gerais Road (Calçada das Escolas Gerais)**, with its small 18th and 19th century buildings. Some have been restored as new apartments and others are still awaiting refurbishment.

Between one mansion and another appears a unique patio, the Pátio dos Quintalinhos, with its iron gate in the high wall. It was here that the "Estudos Gerais" (General Studies) were created, the beginnings in 1290 of the first Portuguese university – an ideal of King Dinis. Inside the patio, which is now occupied by very simple

ESCOLAS GERAIS STREET (RUA DAS ESCOLAS GERAIS)
Tram 28 scrapes by the doors of this narrow street where, in the Pátio dos Quintalinhos, the first Portuguese university was established (left-hand photo below).

SÃO VICENTE ROAD (CALÇADA DE SÃO VICENTE)
The traffic lights regulate the passage of Tram 28 as it shuttles back and forth in the city.

residences, the foundations of this university were found in the last century, though very few traces have remained.

There is also a very attractive blue mansion which is, today, the headquarters of the Naval Petty Officers' Club. Further along, in the **St Vicente Road (Calçada de São Vicente)**, Tram 28 will just manage to scrape by the windows and doors of the little houses that line the narrow cobbled streets. This is where the driver halts the 28, if the traffic lights demand it. They were installed in the 80s to allow the orderly transit of the trams heading for Graça and the on-coming vehicles on their way to Estrela and Prazeres. There used to be signalmen, from the neighbourhood, who used red and green flags to tell the trams when to pass.

On the final bend of Calçada de São Vicente, the white front of the Church and **Monastery of St Vicente de Fora (Igreja e Mosteiro São Vicente de Fora)** comes into view. The buildings to be seen today were constructed on the initiative of King Philip II of Spain, I of Portugal, who laid the foundation stone in 1582. It was designed by the Italian architect Filippo Terzi on the basis of plans by the Spanish royal architect Juan de Herrera, designer of El Escorial, the monumental palace, museum and library complex 45 km from Madrid.

But the first King of Portugal, Afonso Henriques, founded the original Monastery of St Vincent on this spot in Lisbon in 1147, to fulfil a vow he made to the martyr St Vincent for his success in capturing Lisbon from the Moors. That first building was raised on the field where many of the foreign crusaders who helped the king conquer the city lay buried.

The impressive architecture to be admired today is the result of building work that lasted over a century, from 1582 to 1704. On the death of the Italian architect, the work remained in the hands of Portuguese architects, some renowned in their time. One such architect was Baltasar Álvares, who directed the site until 1624.

Within the sober and symmetrical Italian-style frontage, the two bell towers are to be noted, surmounted by lanterns and polygonal domes. Three semi-circular arches with iron gratings stand out in the architecture. The symbols of St Vincent – a palm – and St Sebastian – arrows – are present, in addition to the statues of these two saints and St Augustine (centre) above the entrance.

Other saints have also merited a place in the façade of the church, including St Anthony – who taught here in 1210 – and St Domingos de Gusmão, in the extreme north and south of the first row of niches. In the second row, the figures of St Norbert, on the left, and St Bruno, on the right, flank the three large windows.

Declared a national monument in 1910, the church possesses a noteworthy Iberian organ, which was built in 1765 by the Portuguese organ maker João Fontanes de Maqueixa and restored in 1994 by Claude and Christine Rainolter, from France. It is considered one of the biggest and best examples of 18th-century Portuguese organ building. Unfortunately, the church has been closed since summer 2008 on account of the crumbling mortar and plaster inside.

The Monastery of St Vicente (Mosteiro de São Vicente) beside the church is a most agreeable surprise, with its open atrium – called the Patio of the Orange Trees (Pátio das Laranjeiras), with trees, pergolas, and shaded seats all around. After the ticket office and the café, the visit passes through a small tunnel giving access to the cistern under the West Cloister. Here, it is still possible to see marks of the original 12th-century building.

CHURCH OF ST VICENTE DE FORA (IGREJA DE SÃO VICENTE DE FORA)
The impressive architecture of one of Lisbon's finest churches.

As the visitor ascends the steps, the noble entry to the monastery reveals its wealth of 18th-century decoration, in the Baroque taste of the reign of King João V. On the vaulted plastered-brick ceiling, a painting of the Florentine master Vicenzo Baccherelli portrays the Triumph of St Augustine over heresy, a unique example of tempera painting on a vaulted ceiling surviving in Portugal. All around the walls, original painted-tile panels created by the great master tile-painter Manuel dos Santos, with his technique of smoky blues, presents a nationalist narrative legitimising the House of Bragança, which emerged from the Restoration in 1640. He uses noteworthy figures from the history of Portugal and, in particular, five kings – Afonso Henriques, Sebastian, João IV, Pedro II and João V.

The cloisters are a separate work of art, with their 81 shaped tile-panels, made up of 14,500 pieces by an unknown artist, according to a design from the time of the 16th-century Spanish kings. Landscapes and scenes from fables and sea life are portrayed in every panel, producing lively decoration in an austere building. Stone symbols appear on the panels above the doors around the cloister, representing the arrows of St Sebastian, the canons regular, the bishop's mitre and the symbol of the Order of St Augustine, a heart.

The Mausoleum of the Lisbon Patriarchs (Panteão dos Patriarcas de Lisboa) occupies the former Chapter House. It contains the tombs of the patriarchs since Carlos da Cunha Menezes (1825), though Pope Clement XI created the patriarchate, at the request of King João V, in 1716. Next to this is the Capela dos Meninos de Palhavã, the burial chapel of the sons of King João V that he recognised and made legitimate.

The former refectory of the canons now contains the Mausoleum of the Royal House of Bragança (Panteão dos Reis da Dinastia de Bragança). It holds the impressive tombs of King João V, King Manuel II, who was brought from the United Kingdom, Queen Amélia, the Empress of Brazil, Amélia Eugénia, and the first Emperor of Brazil, Pedro IV (though his mortal remains lie in the Ipiranga Monument in São Paulo, Brazil, following a historic decision by the Portuguese government in 1972). King Carlos I and Prince Luís Filipe, who were shot in 1908 in the Terreiro do Paço also lie there. The architectural setting for the tombs was designed by the famous Portuguese architect Raul Lino (1879-1974).

In the upper storey of the monastery, several areas around the two cloisters were reserved for a very special exhibition – the 38 remarkable painted-tile panels depicting the Fables of La Fontaine. Ordered at the end of the 18th century for the walls in the cloister arches, and recently restored, they form one of the world's greatest concentrations of this ceramic art. From the terrace above this floor, with its decorative pinnacles, there is a beautiful view over the city and the Tagus.

In the last stage of the visit, the sacristy is an extraordinary space with its polychrome inlaid marble walls of magnificent craftsmanship, a bust of King João V and two huge vestment chests in Brazilian jacaranda wood. In addition to all this, there is a fine ceiling painted in oil on canvas, over a wooden base.

Back in the Calçada de São Vicente, it is worth admiring the 17th-century façade of the **Palácio Teles de Menezes**. It was remodelled by the famous Italian architect Nicola Bigaglia, whose work can be seen more or less throughout the country. The mansion has belonged to some important Lisbon families and to a family member of the founder of the oldest Portuguese newspaper, *Diário de Notícias*. The building carries the arms of the Teles de Menezes family on the side and forms the corner of the street that, from here, takes the name 'Voz do Operário'. But before the journey aboard the 28 continues to Graça, it is important to make an incursion into the neighbourhood of the Church of São Vicente de Fora. The street running alongside the church leads to an open space, **Campo de Santa Clara**, the site of Lisbon's oldest market – the **Flea Market (Feira da Ladra)**. It has its origins in the Middle Ages (13th c.), though it has been particularly vibrant since 1552, the time of the Portugal's great maritime and commercial expansion. Every Tuesday and Saturday, from the break of day, countless vendors display their goods for sale on stalls and tables, or even a cloth spread out on the ground.

All manner of yesterday's 'stuff', miscellaneous equipment, old and new clothing, crockery, coins, books, records, CDs, footwear, furniture, photographs and other bric-a-brac can be found there, amid the colourful sight of the people of Lisbon and the many visitors to the city. Right beside the market, from the **Belevedere Botto Machado (Miradouro Botto Machado)**, with its flowerbeds and leafy trees, Lisbon and the Tagus open up magnificently to view.

A short walk from here, by a steep and windy street, lies another important monument – the National Mausoleum (Panteão Nacional). A singular Portuguese Baroque monument, the **National Mausoleum or Church of St Engrácia** has a long history. It began in 1570 when the Infanta Maria (1521-1577) founded the original Church of St Engrácia on this spot, to consolidate the thriving expansion of this urban district. A new parish was established with Pius V's Papal Letter of 1568.

Positioned halfway up the hill, with a view of the Tagus and the surrounding houses, the Church of St Engrácia was the witness of a tragic episode in 1630 when Simão Solis, a "new Christian" (forced convert) was unjustly accused of profaning the sanctuary and, the following year, was burnt alive before the church itself. As the flames wrapped themselves around his body, Simão Solis cried out that just as certainly as he died an innocent man the building works would never end. Years later, it was discovered that someone else committed the theft and the unfortunate Solis had only been there to see his beloved, a novice calls Violante.

True or not, the fact is that the Church took centuries to build – until the second half of the 20th century. First of all, it was decided to build a new chancel in 1632, a slow task that dragged on until 1668 on account of the lack of funds and the outbreak of the War of the Restoration [of Sovereignty]. A new design was requested of the master mason João Antunes, who proved to be the greatest Portuguese architect of the time and who, with the plan drawn up for the new church, was appointed royal architect in 1699.

His innovative design – a building in the form of a Greek cross, containing four arms of equal length, with curving elevations and a hemispheric dome to complete it – revisits the characteristics of the Renaissance. The idea was that this best represented the geometric harmony of the universe, especially with the form of the dome rising towards heaven.

However, the front is closer to traditional Portuguese architecture, recalling the lines used in the neighbouring Church of St Vicente de Fora. Undoubtedly, its originality lies principally in the curving walls – an unprecedented solution in Portugal at the time. These allow special effects of light and shade within the building.

After the death of João Antunes in 1712, the work stopped for over two centuries. It was doubted whether the structure could support

THE BOTTO MACHADO VIEWING TERRACE (MIRADOURO BOTTO MACHADO)
In Campo de Santa Clara, yet another wonderful view over the Tagus.

THE FLEAMARKET (FEIRA DA LADRA)
From the Middle Ages, Lisbon's oldest street market.

NATIONAL MAUSOLEUM (PANTEÃO NACIONAL)
The curving façade of one of the Portuguese capital's most iconic monuments.

The last resting place of great Portuguese personalities, among presidents of the republic, writers and the famous fado singer Amália Rodrigues.

the weight of the dome, though this question was resolved by the French consul in Lisbon, Antoine Duverger. Even so, over the following centuries the work was not resumed, despite many attempts. It was only in the second half of the 20th century, that the Minister of Public Works suggested completing the building. He had the cooperation of various specialists, including the historians Damião Peres and Mário Chicó and the famous architect Raul Lino. The solution adopted was to put two towers into the façade and simplify the dome.

The Church of St Engrácia was classified as a national monument in 1910 and selected as the National Mausoleum. It contains the tombs of great Portuguese personalities, including certain Presidents of the Republic – Teófilo Braga, Sidónio Pais and Óscar Carmona – and writers such as João de Deus, Almeida Garrett and Guerra Junqueiro, in addition to General Humberto Delgado, the opponent of the Estado Novo, and the famous fado singer Amália Rodrigues.

The great figures of Portuguese history are also honoured there with cenotaphs: Luís de Camões – the great poet of the Discoveries; Nuno Álvares Pereira – the Holy Constable; Afonso de Albuquerque – Viceroy of India; Vasco da Gama – the navigator who reached India in 1498; Pedro Álvares Cabral – who discovered Brazil in 1500; and Infante D. Henrique – the driving force behind the epic of the Portuguese maritime accomplishments.

Back along Rua da Voz do Operário, which belongs to two parishes, St Vicente de Fora and Graça, Tram 28 gradually approaches one of its destinations, Graça. But it first passes one of the most emblematic buildings of the 20th century – the **headquarters of The Workers' Voice (A Voz do Operário)**, an educational and charitable society that appeared with the rise of the workers' movement in 1879, a time of struggle against the monarchy. Designed by the architect Manuel Joaquim Norte Jr. between 1912 and 1914, the building is distinctly well-balanced and monumental. It was built thanks to the commitment of important public figures in Lisbon society. Though Art Nouveau in style, its columns are somewhat Neoclassical.

The Tram 28 hurries along Rua da Voz do Operário, as it climbs another hill. It will now arrive at **Graça Square (Largo da Graça)**, this simple square with its trees and its peaceful residents, who meet for a chat in the late afternoon. It used to be vegetable gardens and orchards, and the site of convents and even a few mansions and stately homes. When Tram 28 does not go on to Martin Moniz, another destination on the same line, the terminus is here.

This parish sprang up a long time after the 1755 earthquake and, even then, it only began to define itself with some force in the 19th century. From that time, various examples of **workers' housing quarters or tenements (vilas operárias)** were set up in the vicinity, for example Vila Berta, the Estrela d'Ouro Neighbourhood and Villa Sousa.

Extending from Rua do Sol à Graça to Travessa da Pereira, **Vila Berta** is composed of two and three storey houses with beautiful iron balconies decorated with several vases of colourful flowers. Designed and built in 1902 by Joaquim Francisco Tojal, it was intended for the lower strata of the middle-class, in contrast to the other 'vilas'. **Villa Sousa**, at 82 Largo da Graça, was built in 1890 and the whole of the impressive building's façade is decorated with tiles. The patio – the centre of life in the vila – is surrounded by two and four storey housing units, in addition to the iron gateway.

The **Estrela d'Ouro Neighbourhood**, which stretches from 22 Rua da Graça to 14 Rua Senhora do Monte, is an authentic Lisbon 'vila operária'. It was designed in 1907 by the architect Norte Júnior,

THE VOZ DO OPERÁRIO BUILDING (A VOZ DO OPERÁRIO)
A landmark in the rise of the workers' movement in Lisbon.

WORKERS' HOUSING IN GRAÇA (VILAS OPERÁRIAS NA GRAÇA)
Bairro Estrela d'Ouro and Vila Berta, built from the 19th century onwards.

GRAÇA SQUARE (LARGO DA GRAÇA)
The peaceful square at nightfall, one of the places where Tram 28 ends.

following a commission by the Galician Agapito Serra Fernandes, a great industrialist in the confectionery trade. Created to house his workers, the vila is decorated with stars drawn in the stones of the pavement and the painted-tile panels at the entrance to the neighbourhood. In the middle of the simple houses, arranged in a U-shape around the private streets, named after members of the owner's family, is the house of the Galician industrialist himself, with a lake, garden and private chapel.

Another landmark in this parish is the façade of the former cinema **Royal Cine**, where the first talking picture was projected in Portugal. Though the building is now occupied by a supermarket, it retains some of the features of its golden age, e.g. the stairs, the old clock and the symbol of comedy in the vestibule.

The neighbourhood of Graça has even more secrets to reveal to those who adventure a little beyond the Tram 28 route. For example, near Largo da Graça, there is a beautiful café terrace at the lookout point – **Miradouro Sophia de Mello Breyner Andresen**, with kiosks and yet another view over Lisbon. Behind this lookout point is an Augustinian monastery, founded in 1271 and rebuilt after the 1755 earthquake. It is the **Convent and Church of Graça**: the convent was founded by the hermits of Saint Augustine in the 13th century and the church dates from the 18th century. The whole of the inside is covered with gilt woodcarving, painted tiles and fine ceiling paintings on plaster.

It is worth noting the image of Christ carrying the cross (Senhor dos Passos). This statue belongs to a penitential procession that has taken place on the Second Sunday of Lent for 410 years, without interruption. It used to follow the whole route from the Church of St Roque, in Chiado, to Graça, a route that is being reinstated.

A little further ahead, beyond the Largo da Graça and along Rua Senhora do Monte, the visitor arrives at the chapel and viewing terrace of **Our Lady of the Mount (Capela de Nossa Senhora do Monte or Ermida da Senhora do Monte)**. The original chapel was built very close to the present chapel in 1147, i.e. immediately after the recapture of Lisbon from the Moors. It is dedicated to St Gens of Lisbon, a bishop of the city before the reconquest and a saint who was martyred here.

It was the Augustinian friars who put the saint's stone chair inside the chapel – a chair that started a legend: that pregnant women who sat on it would give birth without complications. Even Queen Maria Ana of Austria, wife of King João V, sat there when she was pregnant with the heir to the throne. The original chapel, however, was destroyed in the earthquake and the present one was built in 1796, a little above the original site, though the chair of St Gens is still there.

The chapel gives on to the fine garden of the **Miradouro da Senhora do Monte**, another special veranda with the beauty of Lisbon at its feet. To the south, the view takes in the whole of the Sea of Straw (part of the River Tagus, so called on account of the flecks of gold that escaped from the Almada mines and shone in the sun, resembling the colour of straw), Castelo São Jorge and a large part of the Baixa Pombalina, and, to the west, the Tagus Estuary, the Bairro Alto skyline and even Monsanto Forest Park.

But for those who feel like continuing the journey on **Tram 28 towards Martim Moniz**, one or two more surprises lie in wait. After travelling down through a series of winding streets, the Tram 28 reaches Avenida Almirante Reis, which marks the opening up of the new city towards the north and the New Avenues (Avenidas Novas).

THE SOPHIA DE MELLO BREYNER ANDRESEN VIEWING TERRACE (MIRADOURO)
The illuminated bust of one of Portugal's most distinguished women poets.

OUR LADY OF THE MOUNT VIEWING TERRACE (MIRADOURO DA SENHORA DO MONTE)
The colours of the late afternoon in Graça and the tile panel identifying the views.

THE CHURCH OF OUR LADY OF HEALTH
(IGREJA DE NOSSA SENHORA DA SAÚDE)
The Pombaline doorway of what became a royal chapel in 1861.

A MANUELINE DOORWAY
In Rua da Mouraria, the unusual entrance to a police station.

MARTIM MONIZ SQUARE (PRAÇA DO MARTIM MONIZ)
A detail of one of the fountains in the city's most multicultural square.

The buildings from the end of the 19th century and the first quarter of the 20th century have Art Nouveau and Art Deco façades. A public fountain – o Chafariz do Desterro – was brought from Largo do Intendente, where it supplied the city. The famous Teatro Rex, with its Neoclassical architecture, is still standing, but the most handsome building on this stretch is the tile-clad façade of the **Viúva Lamego Ceramic Factory (Fábrica Cerâmica Viúva Lamego)**.

In Largo Martim Moniz, Tram 28 really has its last stop, in the square where the multicultural character of the capital can be seen in detail, with its different immigrant communities – Indian, Pakistani, African, Eastern European, Brazilian, Chinese and Asiatic. This square is named in honour of the noble man who, in 1147, wedged his own body in one of the gateways of the Moorish Castle so that King Afonso Henriques' troops could conquer the city.

The fountains in the centre give a certain decorative touch to a square with few significant architectural features, though more careful observation will reveal two small treasures – the **Church of Our Lady of Health (Igreja de Nossa Senhora da Saúde)**, the site of an old chapel built by the Court artillerymen in 1506 in honour of St Sebastian. A Roman soldier and martyr from the end of the third century, he became the saint who gave protection against the evils of the plague, hunger and war.

King Sebastian (1554-1578) had the Church of Saint Sebastian built on the site of the old chapel. In 1570, to combat the pest that was threatening the city again, the first procession in honour of Our Lady of Health took place, an act of devotion that lasted for 340 years, until the Proclamation of the Republic. The procession was only reinstated after 1940, with a new route. The Church of Our Lady of Health, which enjoyed the protection of kings, queens, noblemen and military people, was given royal chapel status in 1861. The building has a Pombaline doorway and, with a very interesting mirror effect, its silhouette is picked out on the pavement in dark stones, a work by artist Eduardo Nery.

A couple of steps further on, in Rua da Mouraria, a police station without parallel comes into view – it is installed in a splendid building with a Manueline doorway, which was probably brought from a chapel. Straight ahead, a sculpture of a Portuguese guitar marks the **Cradle of Fado in the Mouraria neighbourhood (Berço do Fado no Bairro da Mouraria)**. After the conquest of Lisbon, the first king of Portugal assigned this neighbourhood to the Moors. This is where A Severa, the first mythical figure of fado, was born and lived and where Mariza, the most international Portuguese 'fadista' of today, grew up.

Maintaining the musical tradition of the neighbourhood, Tram 28 carries fado singers in the Lisbon Festivities Week in June. From Martim Moniz to Prazeres the tram rolls along to the sound of Portuguese guitars and the well-tuned voices of the female 'fadistas' who, with their black shawls and the posture of a diva, bring back old songs that people know by heart. There is always enthusiastic applause.

FADO ON TRAM 28
'Fadista' singing fado on the tram during the Lisbon Festivities in June.

III. From Baixa to Chiado

It is now necessary to return to Rua da Conceição, in the heart of the historic centre, Baixa Pombalina. From here, Tram 28 travels westwards to Estrela and Prazeres. But, before it arrives there, a lot of interesting history is still to be found in this stretch of the journey – to Chiado, the cosmopolitan neighbourhood of Lisbon. As it leaves Rua da Conceição, the Tram 28 crosses the most famous streets in Baixa – Rua Augusta (the site of the new Museum of Design and Fashion, MUDE), Rua do Ouro, Rua do Crucifixo and Rua Nova do Almada.

Lisbon City Hall (Câmara Municipal de Lisboa or Paços do Conselho) lies roughly a block away from the route. Its iconic triumphal pediment is the work of the French sculptor Anatole Calmels: it contains a sculpture of the arms of the City of Lisbon flanked by a male figure representing Love and Freedom, on the right, with Science and Navigation in the background, and, on the left, a female figure symbolising Freedom, with Trade and Industry in the background.

City Hall was constructed on this site after the 1755 earthquake, to the designs of the architect Eugénio dos Santos Carvalho. In 1863, however, it was completely destroyed by a great fire. It was then rebuilt between 1865 and 1880 in accordance with the plans of a group of professionals, including the architect Domingos Parente da Silva and the engineer Ressano Garcia. Inside, the architect José Luís Monteiro's central staircase is particularly noteworthy. The ornate decoration was carried out by renowned artists such as José Pereira Júnior, Columbano and Malhoa.

 In 1996, the upper floors were damaged by a fire that specially affected the ceilings and the paintings on the first floor. The architect Silva Dias was given the responsibility of the restoration work, which was to be historically and architecturally faithful to

CITY HALL (CÂMARA MUNICIPAL)
City Hall's triumphal pediment, by the French sculptor Anatole Calmels.

the original 19th-century building. From the cast-iron gates of the façade, the space opens up to reveal the staircase and the dome. This is decorated on the inside with chiaroscuro, *trompe-l'oeil* Renaissance motifs and the whole is lit through a glass and iron lantern by António José Burnay.

A first-anniversary plaque commemorating the Proclamation of the Republic in 1910 – an act that has remained associated with this building – can be found on the first landing. It is the work of Simões de Almeida. The Room of the Republic or Golden Room (Sala da República or Sala Dourada) is one of the most beautiful, boasting a ceiling painted with a multicoloured composition of flowers, fruit and garlands by Pereira Júnior and Procópio Ribeiro. The famous Portuguese artist José Malhoa painted the oval medallions representing Music, Singing, the Arts and Literature, and the similarly famous Columbano signed the large round corner medallions showing allegories from Camões, with verses from *The Lusiads* – the greatest work of Luís de Camões, the poet of the Discoveries. The Grand Reception Room (Salão Nobre) has a great wealth of decoration, combining the Neoclassical with the more modern. Particularly noteworthy is the inlaid door by the 18th-century master Leandro Braga, which includes the arms of the City of Lisbon. These have their roots in legend, history and myth going back to the Middle Ages – the ship with two crows, perched fore and aft, represents the arrival of the relics of Saint Vincent the Martyr at Cape St Vincent in the Algarve.

The ceiling painted with allegorical figures by José Rodrigues evokes the symbols of the city, such as navigation, trade and industry, and the Tagus, Renown and the Great Talents. The room is flanked by medallions recalling historical personalities such as Gil Vicente, a jeweller and the founder of Portuguese theatre, and Father António Vieira, a diplomat and eminent preacher, among others.

The square outside displays a **pillory**, a revivalist-style monolithic column composed of ashlar, marble and iron. Built after the 1755 earthquake, the column stands on an octagonal platform and is decorated with lotus flowers and volutes. The shaft consists of three twisted elements forming a spiral, with the inner part left hollow. Crowning the shaft, there is a massive bulb, worked with eight twisted stems and, to complete the whole, a lantern and armillary sphere. This sphere represents the universe – with the Earth occupying the centre. Since the time of King Manuel I, it has been the symbol of the maritime, political and economic power associated with seafaring.

Back at the route of the Tram 28, the driver is preparing to face the steep **St Francis Road (Calçada de São Francisco)**. Gathering speed along the flat ground of Rua da Conceição, the driver presses the button to spray sand on the rails to improve the grip. At the top of the narrow road, a broad view awaits, with a square on the right, Largo da Academia de Belas Artes, and early 19th century bourgeois mansions on the left, in the street now called Vítor Cordon. Two of these are worth noting – the Palácio Ribeira Grande, nowadays the school and premises of the CGTP (General Confederation of Portuguese Workers), which is surmounted by four statues symbolising the seasons, and the Palácio Conde de Monsaraz, the poet Conde de Monsaraz' home.

After a tight curve, Tram 28 enters Rua dos Duques de Bragança. This is the title (Duke of Bragança) of the present heir to the Portuguese throne, Dom Duarte.

CITY HALL (CÂMARA MUNICIPAL)
The pillory in front of City Hall and a modern design using traditional Portuguese mosaic, by Eduardo Nery.

ST FRANCIS ROAD (CALÇADA DE SÃO FRANCISCO)
The tram 28 at the top of one the most steep hills of Lisbon.

What immediately attracts the visitor's attention are the distinctive dark-green iron staircases set against the yellow walls – they are **the fire escape of São Luiz Municipal Theatre (escadaria de incêndio do Teatro Municipal São Luiz)**. The main entrance is on the street above, Rua Antonio Maria Cardoso. The new theatre was opened in 1894 under the name 'Teatro Dona Amélia', in the presence of King Carlos I and Queen Amélia, its patroness. It was the idea of the actor Guilherme da Silveira, who managed to bring together numerous investors, including Viscount São Luiz de Braga, the driving force behind the project.

The theatre was designed by the French architect Louis Reynaud, who gave it a cosmopolitan and Parisian air. After the fall of the monarchy and the flight of the royal family in 1910, it took the name 'Teatro da República'. However, after a fire destroyed it completely four years later, the viscount commissioned the architect Tertuliano Marques to rebuild it as it had been.

In 1928, the theatre became a cinema, under the name 'São Luiz Cine', showing Fritz Lang's film *Metropolis* on the first night. Two years later it was remodelled and became the first talking picture cinema in Portugal. In the following decades, cinema audiences dwindled and, in 1971, it was acquired by Lisbon City Hall, once again changing its name, this time to Teatro Municipal São Luiz. After years of indeterminate programming, the theatre is now a key reference in the cultural life of the city and, especially, Chiado. It also possesses a studio theatre, *café concert* and restaurant.

On the other side of the street, the main opera house in Lisbon, **S. Carlos National Theatre (Teatro Nacional de São Carlos)**, takes up a full side of the square where the great poet Fernando Pessoa was born. It was inaugurated in 1793 by Queen Maria I, replacing the Teatro Ópera do Tejo, which was destroyed in 1755 earthquake. It was built in just six months, according to the design of the architect José da Costa e Silva, who derived his inspiration from the great European theatres like San Carlo in Naples, for the interiors, and Alla Scala in Milan, for both the façade and the interior.

The theatre was inaugurated in 1793 with Domenico Cimarosa's opera *La Ballerina Amante*; years later, in 1958, the diva Maria Callas sang *La Traviata* here, to a dazzled Lisbon audience. It was also here that the emperor and tribal leader of Mozambique, Gungunhana, was presented as a war trophy. He had been defeated in his revolt against Portuguese colonial rule in 1895 and was brought to Lisbon in irons by Mouzinho de Albuquerque.

The work advanced in 1792 – during a time that was hardly open to the ideas of the Enlightenment – thanks to the activity of a group of 40 important Lisbon merchants, including the Quintela family. They already played an important role in theatre affairs following the creation of the Society for the Support of Public Theatres. It was also thanks to Police Superintendent Pina Manique. The project only became possible when it had a charity as a source of income – Casa Pia, which was founded by Pina Manique in 1780.

The auditorium, richly decorated by the Italian Giovanni Appiani, retains the aristocratic atmosphere of the times, especially with the five rows of boxes and the impressive royal box, rare in public theatres since the 18th century. A veritable gem of late Baroque theatre architecture, the room underwent various changes in the 19th and 20th centuries, though it has maintained all the beauty and ability to impress from its first days.

THEATRE SÃO LUIZ (TEATRO SÃO LUIZ)
Spectacular fire escapes on one of the theatre's walls, designed by the French architect Louis Reynaud.

Great Italian companies were presented here – the reason why the theatre was also called the Italian Theatre. All compositions, even by Portuguese composers, had to be in Italian. Nowadays, the opera season runs from June to November and, in the summer, there are special presentations in the theatre square, with open-air music, dance and theatre performances.

Straight opposite the theatre, in that yellow building with its wrought iron balconies, one of the greatest poets of the Portuguese language, **Fernando Pessoa**, was born on 13 June 1880. A plaque commemorates his birth at 4 Largo de São Carlos (4th floor, left-hand flat). A statue in the square by the Belgian sculptor Jean Michel Folon, unveiled in 2008, also makes reference to the poet, who was considered one of the most representative of the 20th century.

His father was a music critic for the newspaper *Diário de Notícias* and wrote a huge amount on the performances at the National Theatre of São Carlos. His mother, who was from the Azores, took care of the house. But Pessoa's life changed when he was only five years old. Following his father's death, his mother remarried and the family moved to Durban, South Africa.

The poet's full name was Fernando António Nogueira Pessoa, in honour of the popular saint of Lisbon, St Anthony, who was born on the same day. He was christened near by in Rua Garrett, in the **Basilica of the Martyrs (Basílica dos Mártires)**. The parish church of Our Lady of the Martyrs was created in 1147, after King Afonso Henriques had captured Lisbon from the Moors, and was dedicated to the English, French and German crusaders who lost their lives in this battle. From a small chapel, it became a Baroque church, which was destroyed in the 1755 earthquake but immediately rebuilt in all its glory.

In the baptistery, an impressive double-door in ironwork carries the inscription: "The first christening after Lisbon was taken from the Moors in the year 1147 took place in this parish." The church is richly decorated with painted ceilings and individual chapels with gilded woodcarving. It possesses chased silver candelabra, the remarkable work of Lisbon silversmiths, and an 18th-century nativity scene with 126 figures, from the school of Machado de Castro.

Fernando Pessoa always remembered the tolling of the church bells – "Oh bell of my village, sorrowful in the quiet afternoon, / Each time you strike / it resounds within my soul." A passionate lover of Lisbon, Pessoa never left the city again, to the day he died in 1935 following a complication caused by gall stones and cirrhosis of the liver. According to the family, his last words were written in English, "I know not what tomorrow will bring."

A discreet person, educated in English schools in Durban, South Africa, the poet lived in Lisbon as a translator of business correspondence, though he also worked with prominent periodicals associated with the Modernist movement of the time, e.g. *Athena*, *Orpheu* and *Presença*. Simultaneously, in his poetic works, he created an enigmatic list of heteronyms that assumed different ideologies, styles, thoughts and lyric aspects. One of the most famous sentences from one of his semi-heteronyms, Bernardo Soares, in the *Book of Disquiet*, asserts, "My country is the Portuguese language."

The main heteronyms emanating from his incredible imagination were Álvaro de Campos – the naval engineer who travelled around the East and wrote *Opiário* and the famous poem *Tabacaria*, among others, Ricardo Reis – the pro-monarchy doctor

NATIONAL THEATRE OF SÃO CARLOS (TEATRO NACIONAL DE SÃO CARLOS)
The elegance of the main opera house in Lisbon.

SÃO CARLOS SQUARE
(LARGO DE SÃO CARLOS)
The house where the poet Fernando Pessoa was born.

who went into exile in Brazil in 1919, and Alberto Caeiro – the peasant with no occupation and almost no education, whom Pessoa considered his master. He wrote a famous line: "There is quite a lot of metaphysics in not thinking about anything."

Then there was Pessoa himself, the lone and melancholy poet, who took existential angst and the disquietude over the indecipherable enigma of life and transferred them into sublime words. There is a famous line from his poem *Autopsicografia*, written in 1931: "Poets are pretenders. They pretend so completely that they manage to pretend that the pain they really feel is pain."

Fernando Pessoa joined in the bubbling cultural bustle that took place in Chiado, especially in the **Café A Brasileir**a, which opened in 1905 and became the meeting point of early 20th-century intellectuals, artists and politicians. People like the painter Almada Negreiros (who also created the very fine stained glass in the Church of the Holy Constable – Igreja do Santo Condestável – in Prazeres, also served by Tram 28) were regulars at this century-old café, which continues to draw in the cosmopolitan public that circulates in the streets of the neighbourhood today. Chiado was restored after the terrible fire in 1988, in accordance with the general plan of one of Portugal's greatest architects, Álvaro Siza Vieira. Pessoa's connection with this café was such that a bronze statue by Lagoa Henriques was erected in his honour on the café terrace. The café itself was completely decorated with works of art by prominent Portuguese modern artists such as Almada Negreiros, Eduardo Viana and Bernardo Marques. These were replaced by artists representing the various trends in the Lisbon artistic scene of the 1970s, such as Vespeira, Noronha da Costa, João Hogan and Eduardo Nery, among others.

In the Café A Brasileira is where the word 'bica' was coined, to describe the tasting and testing of genuine Brazilian coffee, which was a novelty in Lisbon at the beginning of the 20th century. The interior retains the original lines of those times, with its large oak Renaissance-style counter, gilt woodcarving and wall mirrors. The marble-topped tables recall the many thinkers who came here for their regular literary gatherings or to engage in heated political discussion. In one such episode, the painter Almada Negreiros read his *Anti-Dantas Manifesto*, a text that severely criticised the prevailing cultural and artistic scene and, in fact, opened the way to the Futurist movement in Portugal.

All over Chiado and Baixa there are reminders of Pessoa, the discreet and genial poet who did the rounds of the cafés and restaurants after work – Martinho da Arcada in Terreiro do Paço, the restaurant Pessoa in Rua dos Dourados, Rossio cafés that no longer exist, like Café Suíço, and the restaurants A Licorista, and Val do Rio, where he was photographed having a drink. This was one of his regular habits and must have contributed to the health problems that led to his death in 1935.

A year before Pessoa's death, his only published book appeared – *Mensagem*. It extolled Portuguese sentiment, alluding to Sebastianism, the mystical movement proclaiming the return of King Sebastian, who died at the Battle of Alcácer-Quibir in 1578. Pessoa left a large legacy of unpublished work, kept as loose sheets in the famous chest that he had in his last home, at 16 Rua Coelho da Rocha in Campo de Ourique, today the Fernando Pessoa House (Casa Fernando Pessoa) whih is near one of the Tram 28 stops on the way to Prazeres.

The poet actually used Tram 28 – and 25, which runs from Prazeres to Rua da Alfândega in Baixa – to travel between the offices where he worked in Baixa, the cafés in Chiado and Rossio and the various houses where he lived, renting simple rooms. But the Café-Restaurant Martinho da Arcada, known at the time as Café da Arcada, was his usual perch in the final years and operated as his personal office.

This was where he sat at his table for hours, deep in thought, writing and drinking 'bicas' (coffee) and 'bagaços' (a spirit), in such oblivion that he stayed after the café had closed and sometimes even shared the owners' dinner. But on most nights the restaurant owners (the Sá Mourão family) had to insist that he eat. They even invented an *Omelette Pessoa* – in fact, fried eggs with cheese – to force him to consume something more substantial.

It was in Café-Restaurant Martinho da Arcada that Pessoa (Bernardo Soares) wrote the beautiful sentence from the Book of Disquiet: "In the long afternoons of summer, I love the calm of the low town (historic centre)." Here, too, his friend Almada Negreiros once found him hiding under the table, afraid of a heavy thunderstorm that lifted the waves of the Tagus over the steps of Quay of the Columns (Cais das Colunas).

But Pessoa always returned to Chiado, this neighbourhood of his birth, this magnet in the 19th century for the illustrious and vain bourgeoisie of Lisbon, who paraded their coats and top hats and embroidered Parisian dresses. The Chiado that saw the first electric lights installed in 1878. The Chiado of the fashionable cafés and pastry shops like Pastelaria Bénard, established in 1800. The Chiado of elegant shops, traditional jewellers, deluxe hotels, bookshops and sophisticated restaurants – like Tavares, the oldest in Portugal. In the 220 years of its history it has been the meeting point of political and cultural elites and international personalities such as King Humberto of Italy, Eisenhower and Fellini, among others who have passed there, 37 Rua da Misericórdia.

This Chiado, which the Portuguese writer Eça de Queiroz (1845-1900) – one of the most important Portuguese authors, a precursor of Realism in Portugal – mentioned in one of his books, *As Prosas Bárbaras*, saying: "Even the mud here is high quality." Eça, whose work exists in around twenty languages, wrote well-known novels like The Maias, Cousin Basil and The Crime of Father Amaro. He was a fierce critic of the Lisbon middle classes and the conservatism of the Church.

In Cousin Basil, published in 1878, Eça de Queiroz makes a ferocious attack on 19th-century urban middle-class society, and the Lisbon middle classes in particular. In this narrative, he presents three main characters – Luísa, a young, romantic and adulterous wife, who repents in the end; Jorge, the devoted husband; and the seducer Cousin Basil, an irresponsible dandy and ladykiller with an aristocratic and decadent way of life. This work, Eça hoped, would be an instrument of social resistance, in which the middle classes, the main readers, would recognize their own defects and rectify them.

In **Largo Barão de Quintela**, a square in Rua do Alecrim – this street, just ahead, that gazes over the Tagus, in an urban corridor lined by 19th-century mansions and contemporary buildings – there is a statue to the great Portuguese writer just mentioned, Eça de Queiroz. Under António Teixeira Lopes' stone sculptures depicting the writer and an allegory of Truth, a female figure, there is a quotation from his work: "Over the firm nakedness of truth, the diaphanous robe of fantasy".

FERNANDO PESSOA
One of the famous pictures of the intriguing Portuguese poet.

CAFÉ A BRASILEIRA
Opened in 1905, A Brasileira has always been a meeting point for intellectuals and artists..

THE BRONZE STATUE OF FERNANDO PESSOA

In honour of the poet, a regular at the café A Brasileira.

Now the bell of Tram 28 echoes as it crosses **Largo do Chiado**. This curious name goes back to the year 1567 and may refer to the screeching of the wagon wheels that passed here or, again, to the nickname of the 16th century poet of the people and ex-friar, António do Espírito Santo, the Screeching Poet (Poeta Chiado). He is represented here in a statue by the sculptor Costa Mota, almost opposite the Café A Brasileira. Or it may be a reference to the 16th-century innkeeper, Gaspar Dias, called Chiado, who owned a tavern where the Armazéns do Chiado stand today, at the end of Rua Garrett. This street is another literary reference in this neighbourhood, this time to the poet and writer Almeida Garrett.

Close to Rua Garrett lies **Largo do Carmo**, a square with long-established jacarandas, an 18th-century public fountain and the ruins of **Carmo Monastery (Convento do Carmo)**, with its transversal Gothic arches still standing as a symbolic witness of the 1755 earthquake. An archaeological museum keeps the memory of the place alive, with a collection of tombs, statues, inscriptions, heraldic pieces, ceramics and coins, in addition to a 14th-century baptismal font, an Arab basin from Penha Longa Convent and even 19th-century painted tiles.

Built in the 14th century by Constable Nuno Álvares Pereira (the Holy Constable, canonised in 2009) to fulfil a promise made on the battlefield of Aljubarrota in 1385, the monastery was occupied by Carmelite Friars. It was the main Gothic church in the Portuguese capital. With regard to the Holy Constable himself, there is a church dedicated to him on the road to Prazeres.

The old monastery building houses the Carmo Barracks of the National Republican Guard (GNR), where the President of the Council Marcello Caetano took shelter in the heat of the Revolution of 25 April 1974. This was the main stage, as it was here that the Estado Novo surrendered to the Armed Forces Movement. Tanks occupied the square and a crowd of people gathered, in the presence of one of the leaders of the Carnation Revolution, Captain Salgueiro Maia. The regime fell without a single drop of blood.

One of the emblematic monuments of Chiado is very close – the **Santa Justa Elevator (Elevador de Santa Justa)**. This incredible neo-Gothic iron construction, decorated with fine tracery, was built at the turn of the 19th and 20th centuries by Raoul Mesnier du Ponsard, a Portuguese engineer of French origin. The elevator has connected Largo do Carmo to the historic centre, Baixa Pombalina, since 1902. After running on steam in its first years of operation, it started to use electrical power in 1907.

A little further ahead, in one of the side streets at the top of Rua Garrett, the National Museum of Contemporary Art, more commonly known as **Chiado Museum (Museu Nacional de Arte Contemporânea, Museu do Chiado)** is installed – more precisely, at 4-6 Rua Serpa Pinto. It exhibits an art collection from the second half of the 19th century to the present day.

Chiado also boasts the two beautiful Baroque churches, the **Church of Our Lady of the Incarnation (Igreja de Nossa Senhora da Encarnação) and Loreto Church or the Church of the Italians (Igreja do Loreto, Igreja dos Italianos)**, implanted on the two corners of the street that, to the south, is called Rua do Alecrim and, to the north, Rua da Misericórdia. Loreto Church was consecrated in 1552 and belonged to the Italian community in the Portuguese capital. It was the first large-scale

CHIADO SQUARE (LARGO DO CHIADO)
Another moment of light on the streets of Chiado.

THE RUINS OF CARMO MONASTERY (CONVENTO DO CARMO)
The precious details in stone at the Archaeological Museum in Carmo Monastery
and the transversal Gothic arches that still stand as an emblematic witness of the 1755 earthquake.

SANTA JUSTA ELEVATOR (ELEVADOR DE SANTA JUSTA)
The Neogothic tracery embellishing this 19th-century iron construction.

CHIADO MUSEUM (MUSEU DO CHIADO)
Contemporary art in Chiado.

**THE CHURCH OF OUR LADY OF THE INCARNATION
(IGREJA DE NOSSA SENHORA DA ENCARNAÇÃO)**
The Neoclassical façade reconstructed in the Pombaline period

LORETO CHURCH (IGREJA DO LORETO)
Or the Church of the Italians, consecrated in 1552.

structure to be built over the **Fernandine Walls (Muralha Fernandina)** – the new city walls built between 1373 and 1377 by Fernando I. Remains of the wall may be seen inside the shopping centre at 14 Rua da Misericórdia.

This Mannerist church suffered a serious fire in 1651. It has been restored on various occasions, including after the 1755 earthquake. The fabulous ceiling with a mural painted on wooden planks has been restored; the floor and walls of the church and the twelve side-chapels representing the twelve apostles are clad in Italian marble; and there is an 18th-century pipe organ. Of note in the main façade is the image of our Lady of Loretto and papal arms flanked by two angels, the work of the Italian artist Francesco Borromini.

Directly opposite, the Church of Our Lady of the Incarnation has a Neoclassical façade with Rococo decorative elements and images of St Catherine, which belonged to the old mediaeval gate. The sober interior has a simple nave with a fine painted ceiling by Pedro Alexandrino. The church constructed on the southern flank of the former St Catherine's Gate in the Fernandine Walls was greatly damaged in the earthquake and was reconstructed in accordance with the Marquis of Pombal's standard model for ecclesiastical architecture.

At the top of Rua da Misericórdia there is also the **Church of St Roque (Igreja de São Roque)** and its museum. This remarkable church, with its Mannerist architecture and Baroque and Rococo interior decoration, was built by the Jesuits in the 16th century. It was given to the charitable organisation Misericórdia de Lisboa in 1762, when the Company of Jesus was suppressed by the Marquis of Pombal.

The splendour of the interior is particularly notable, with different artworks and architectural lines that served as a reference for the dissemination of Portuguese religious architecture in Brazil, India and the Far East in the 16th and 17th centuries.

The chancel and pulpit are decorated with different kinds of Italian marble and an engraved silver and bronze light-holder. The various side chapels, covered in gilt woodcarving, are to be noted, in particular the chapel of Our Lady of Mercy (Nossa Senhora da Piedade), with its inlaid marble and decorative woodcarving, and the chapel of St John the Baptist (São João Batista), which King John V had decorated with marble and lapis lazuli in the first half of the 18th century. He commissioned the Italian architects Luigi Vanvitelli and Nicola Salvi to carry out the work.

The Museum of São Roque was set up in the former Professed House of the Company of Jesus. It is connected to the church and has a collection of over 300 works of art, including exuberant Baroque paintings in polychrome wood, intricate reliquaries, liturgical vestments and other church treasures – for example, two large engraved silver torch holders by the Italian artist Giuseppe Gagliardi. The permanent exhibition is divided into five sections and contains the relics of St Roque, which gave rise to the construction of the original chapel in 1506, works of art displaying oriental influence, and artistic objects that tell the history of the institution itself.

MISERICÓRDIA SQUARE (LARGO DA MISERICÓRDIA)
The bronze figure of the lottery ticket seller in front of St Roque Museum, which has a valuable collection of sacred art.

IV. Praça Luís de Camões and Other Hills

Luís de Camões Square (Praça Luís de Camões) is another Chiado landmark. It commemorates the greatest poet in the Portuguese language, who transformed Vasco da Gamma's Lusitanian sea epic into perfect verse in *The Lusiads*, his greatest work. He describes the passage round the Cape of Torments (Cabo das Tormentas), the present-day Cape of Good Hope, in South Africa, and the discovery of the sea route to India. Vítor Bastos' 4-metre statue of the poet stands on a stone plinth 7.5 metres high – but his laurel-crowned head does not reveal the sad and turbulent life he led or his death in poverty.

Reports of his troubled youth in Portugal tell of his Dominican and Jesuit education, his love for women at Court, even King Manuel's sister, and his life of brawling and dissipation. He lost his right eye in a battle against the Moors in Ceuta in 1549, returning to Lisbon an embittered man.

Camões (c. 1524-1580) went to Goa in India – after a brawl in Rossio, followed by his arrest, a royal pardon and his subsequent release – where he wrote the main part of his poem. At the same time he was taking part in military expeditions with the Portuguese fleets in the East and the Persian Gulf. He was appointed chief superintendent of the deceased in the region of China, with the responsibility of provisionally administrating their estates. He lived in a cave in Macau, where he wrote a fair part of *The Lusiads*. When he was shipwrecked near the River Mekong on the Cambodian coast, he saved the manuscript of the poem, quite heroically, but lost his Chinese companion, Dinamene. He would remember her in various sonnets. After this episode, he stayed in the region in the company of Buddhist monks, for some time.

On returning to India, he was imprisoned for debt and, during the return voyage to Portugal, he called in at the Isle of

LUÍS DE CAMÕES SQUARE (PRAÇA LUÍS DE CAMÕES)
The statue of the poet who sang the epic story of the Portuguese Discoveries.
The square that divides the cosmopolitanism of Chiado from the alternative modernity of Bairro Alto.

Mozambique, where he lived for over two years, dependent on the kindness of friends. When he finally returned to Lisbon in 1570, he ended his days in sickness and penury, since the meagre three-yearly pension granted by the young King Sebastian was not sufficient to live on. He died at his mother's side in a simple house in Mouraria, in 1579, when the plague was sweeping Lisbon, and was buried in Santana Convent, with the simple funeral paid for by the Company of Courtiers. His supposed mortal remains lie in a splendid tomb in Jerónimos Monastery.

The first two editions of *The Lusiads* were published in 1572, while the poet was still alive. There were only two hundred copies, full of printing errors. In 1584, the third edition was expurgated by the censor, who deleted various lines indiscriminately on religious grounds – a situation that continued until the fourth edition in 1609. But his words will last forever:

> *The arms and the distinguished heroes*
> *Who, from Lusitania's western shore,*
> *Over seas hitherto unsailed*
> *Ventured beyond Taprobana itself,*
> *Through testing perils and wars,*
> *Beyond the limits of human strength,*
> *And among distant peoples built*
> *The new kingdom they so much extolled.*

The plinth is surrounded by eight representatives of Portuguese classical culture – the cosmographer Pedro Nunes, the three historians Fernão Lopes, Fernão Lopes de Castanheda and João de Barros, the chronicler Gomes Eanes de Azurara and three poets:

Francisco Sá Menezes, Jerónimo Corte-Real and Vasco Quevedo Castello-Branco. The monument was erected between 1860 and 1867. The square itself was laid out in 1859, after the removal of the ruins of the old Palace of the Marquis of Marialva, a cluster of little houses occupying the site.

This is the second most important statue in Lisbon, after that of King José I in Terreiro do Paço. It is said that Pedro V, who died in 1861, laid the foundation stone. In the 1880 celebrations marking the tri-centenary of the poet's death, in the fervour of the festivities, some romantic artists even committed suicide. As the story goes, the statue was covered in mourning for Portugal, because of the British Ultimatum.

Through this square, Largo de Camões, with its fully restored century-old **Refreshment Kiosk (Quiosque de Refresco)**, the trams of Line 28 wind their way towards Estrela and Prazeres – or to Graça. It is almost a ritual stop here, on top of one of the hills of Lisbon. This hill is the crossroads between the cosmopolitanism of Chiado and the tradition and alternative modernity of **Bairro Alto**, this stronghold of Lisbon night life. Bairro Alto is made up of narrow lanes full of restaurants, fado houses and bars that share the scant space with elderly residents, young designers, and journalists from one of the only newspapers – the sporting daily *A Bola* – that have survived in the neighbourhood.

At the end of the 15th century, it was the site of olive groves, vineyards and vegetable gardens, before becoming the property of the Jewish physician, surgeon and court astrologist Guedelha Palaçano. It was divided into plots and sold to the first inhabitants – sailors, merchants and craftsmen – who were later joined by clergymen, sea captains, aristocrats and the middle class.

In the 16th century, the neighbourhood already boasted straight streets, which were suitable for coaches, the means of transport for the upper class. There were social gatherings and balls in the mansions. Right beside them the first taverns also appeared, with their disagreements and brawls. Even with the 1755 earthquake, the 16th-century urban fabric was retained.

Later, in the 19th century and first quarter of the 20th century, Bairro Alto became the centre of Lisbon journalism. It contained the editorial offices of important newspapers like the *Diário de Notícias*, which gave its name to one of the streets. It was always a Bohemian quarter, a characteristic that it has maintained to the present day, with its wide variety of bars and restaurants.

Tram 28 continues its journey towards Estrela and Prazeres, with the driver preparing to pass along Rua do Loreto and across **Largo do Calhariz**, which belongs to two parishes, Santa Catarina and São Paulo. In the 15th century, this whole area between Largo do Camões and Calhariz was a secluded spot with olive groves, outside the city walls. This only changed when the rural properties existing there were broken up.

Many of the mansions from that time can still be admired, e.g. the **Palácio Valada-Azambuja**, which was destroyed in the earthquake and rebuilt over 200 years. It now houses the **Camões Municipal Library (Biblioteca Municipal Camões)**. Directly opposite there is the **Palácio Sobral**, which had a long and interesting history before it was transformed into the offices of one of the main Portuguese banks.

Built between 1770 and 1780, this mansion was the scene of concerts and festivities, especially the sumptuous festivities honouring the birth of the Princess of Beira, Maria Teresa, in 1793.

Portuguese and foreign singers such as Luísa Todi, Violanti, Angelleli and Ferracuti were invited. On the same day, a few blocks from there, the Teatro Nacional de São Carlos was inaugurated, in honour of the first daughter of King João VI and Queen Carlota Joaquina.

An arch links this mansion to **Palácio do Sousa Calharizes**, which gave its name to the square and is also part of the bank's premises. Built in the 18th century, the mansion has also been the residence of a famous diplomat, Pedro de Sousa Holstein, and the headquarters of the Ministry of Foreign Affairs, in 1882.

In 1947, a bank bought the mansion. It carried out various alterations to connect it to the neighbouring mansion with an arch, thus creating a single architectural ensemble. In 1997, the mansion underwent new restoration work, for which it was awarded the Eugénio dos Santos Prize.

In the narrow street that follows Largo (Square) de Calhariz, which is not really a square in the strict sense of the word but rather a notion of a square, inspired by the mansions around it, Tram 28 also passes cafés, fruit shops and florists before giving its passengers a glimpse of a very typical lift in the city – the **Bica Elevator (Elevador da Bica)**.

The Bica Elevator, another of Lisbon's monuments, is a funicular that manages to climb one of the steepest streets in the city – Rua da Bica de Duarte Belo, which connects Largo do Calhariz and Rua de São Paulo. Opened in 1892, it is the most characteristic elevator in the capital and one of the neighbourhood's tourist attractions. It was designed by Raoul Mesnier du Ponsard, the Portuguese engineer of French origin who designed the Santa Justa Elevator in Chiado.

BICA ELEVATOR (ELEVADOR DA BICA)
On one of Lisbon's steepest slopes, a funicular from the 1890s

Originally, the elevator was operated by a water counterweight system – the passenger car that began the descent filled the water tank installed in the canopy and with the force resulting from this weight, in combination with the gravity of the slope, pulled the ascending carriage. It was later equipped with a tramway-cab system and, from 1896, operated on steam. It was only electrified in 1914, though in that year an accident happened that put the elevator out of service for nine years.

Today, the yellow elevator, matching Tram 28, plies the slope between 7 am and 9 pm, from Monday to Saturday, and 9 am to 9 pm on Sundays and public holidays. It is worth noting that the street, which is full of small, simple buildings, has become another centre of Lisbon night life, with the opening of various bars on the steep incline.

With its public fountains, a reminder of a water conduit from earlier times, the Bica neighbourhood is also the setting for important celebrations in June, at the time of the City Festivities and the 'people's marches'. It has won this contest seven times since 1952. In addition, it is the home of writers and fado singers such as the veteran Carlos do Carmo.

The lane parallel to the Bica Elevator has a viewing terrace – **Miradouro do Alto de Santa Catarina** – that is almost hidden within the neighbourhood, in a space that once marked the limit between town and country. Towards sunset, the splendid view of the River Tagus opening out in front is one of the best, with the tones of the 25 April Bridge changing as the sunlight strikes it at the end of the day.

The viewing terrace, with its garden and spreading trees, has a **statue of Adamastor** – the figure created by the poet Luís de Camões in *The Lusiads* to describe the terrible Cape of Good Hope in South Africa, the former Cape of Torments, which offered a formidable passage in the discovery of the sea route to India. This has been a special lookout point for observing the Tagus and the south bank since the 16th century, when it was called Monte do Pico or Belvedere. From here, people watched the shipping on the river, which gave rise to the popular saying "Watching the shipping from Alto de Santa Catarina" (or waiting for something that can or will never arrive).

After breathing in the indescribable blue of the Tagus and admiring this translucent light that falls over Lisbon, transforming it every hour of the day, every step of the way, it is time to return to Tram 28 and travel down **Calçada do Combro**. Other great mansions are to be seen, for example, the Palácio do Correio Velho. Today it is an auction house but it has been a warehouse, editorial office, the headquarters of the General Confederation of Labour and, in the first part of the 1800s, the headquarters of the General Post Office, hence its name, Correio Velho (Old Post Office).

Just as the incline becomes more pronounced, the fine and impressive façade of the **Church of St Catherine or the Church of the Paulists (Igreja de Santa Catarina or Igreja dos Paulistas)** comes into view. In the 16th century, Queen Catarina of Austria, wife of King João III, built the original church on the heights of the parish of St Catherine. In 1755, it was lost in the earthquake. Situated now in the former monastery, Convento do Santíssimo Sacramento dos Religiosos Paulistas da Serra de Ossa, which was established in 1647, the 17th-century church is one of the most important places of worship in Lisbon, with its monumental façade, twin towers, spacious porch and opulent interior.

THE ALTO DE SANTA CATARINA VIEWING TERRACE (MIRADOURO DO ALTO DE SANTA CATARINA)
The splendid view of the Tagus is even more spectacular at the end of the day, when the 25 April Bridge takes on a special radiance.

COMBRO ROAD (CALÇADA DO COMBRO)
The grand façade of the Church of St Catherine, or the Paulists, consecrated in 1647.

THE CHURCH OF OUR LADY OF MERCIES (IGREJA DE NOSSA SENHORA DAS MERCÊS)
A glimpse of the incredible architecture of the church that replaced the old chapel dedicated to the Mother of Heaven.

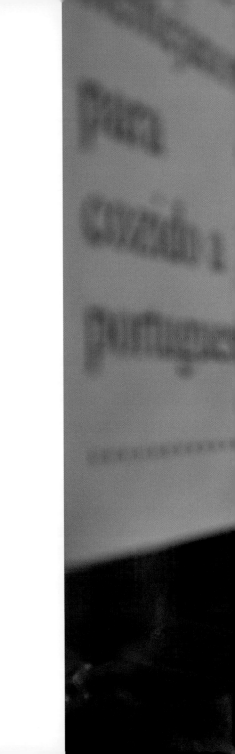

STREET OF THE BLACK PEOPLE'S WELL (RUA DO POÇO DOS NEGROS)
The narrow street where there was probably a well for Benedictine friars, who wore black habits.

The high altar is composed of an enormous altarpiece in carved and gilded wood. Commissioned in 1727, it was the last example of an important set of large-scale Portuguese Baroque gilded altarpieces that the master Santos Pacheco carved to adorn the high altars of various churches in Lisbon. Solomonic columns on corbels, supported by figures of angels, provide the framework for the high altar and the beautiful painted stucco ceiling by the Italian Giovanni Grossi enhances the noble atmosphere of this church. The high altar also contains sculptures of St Paul the Hermit, St Catherine – a martyr who lived in Egypt, where she died around the year 305, during the persecutions of Diocletian – and St Anthony of Egypt. They are probably of Flemish origin. In addition to the other chapels around the nave, it is worth noting the magnificent organ decorated with the figures of child musicians, an outstanding Baroque piece dating from 1730-1740.

The whole church is decorated with important paintings, especially by Vieira Lusitano. His panels of hermit saints can be seen in the transept. Other canvasses represent the Evangelists and Doctors of the Church – between the chapel arches – and the cardinal virtues – above the arches at the entrance and below the upper choir. The upper choir also contains paintings of the life of St Paul the Hermit, in twelve brightly coloured panels from the workshop of André Gonçalves, one of the most important painters in 18th-century Portugal.

Tram 28 then proceeds to Largo Dr. António de Sousa de Macedo, a space in a triangle of streets that includes Rua do Poço dos Negros (Street of the Black People's Well) – where there was probably a well for the black-habited Benedictine monks. Tram 28 comes from that side on the way to Graça. Before the journey continues, it is important to note an ornate church at the top of Travessa do Convento de Jesus – **Igreja de Nossa Senhora das Mercês**, an impressive building that gives onto Largo de Jesus. The flight of stone steps, the large two-storey façade, the double-curved arch and the oval medallion showing Our Lady of Jesus were part of the design by Joaquim de Oliveira and Mateus Vicente de Oliveira in the reconstruction after the earthquake. In the 16th century, the place where the church stands was uncultivated land given to the Third Order of St Frances, which already contained a small chapel dedicated to the Mother of Heaven. The monks then founded the Monastery of Our Lady of Jesus in 1595, funding it with alms.

Of particular interest in the cruciform design are the transept, with its two elaborate altars decorated with gilded woodcarving on a marble front crowned with the arms of Portugal, and a set of twelve 17th-century paintings of the steps in the life of St Francis of Assisi, attributed to the artist Marcos da Cruz. The ceiling contains a painting of Our Lady of Mercies (Nossa Senhora das Mercês), the present patron of the church, and, at the sides, there are 14 decorated chapels and two painted-wood pulpits in João V style. The Passage Room is decorated with a remarkable set of blue and white tiles by Oliveira Bernardes, from around 1715, one of the best examples of Baroque tilework in Portugal.

Once again, the Tram 28 passes through narrow streets and seems almost to brush the windows of the houses. Rua dos Poiais de São Bento joins Calçada da Estrela and Tram 28 ascends a pronounced incline to reach a level area from which the **Assembly of the Republic (Assembleia da República)** rises majestically. Also called the Palace of São Bento, this former Benedictine monastery

THE PORTUGUESE PARLIAMENT (ASSEMBLEIA DA REPÚBLICA OR PALÁCIO DE SÃO BENTO)
The 16th-century Benedictine monastery is now the seat of political power in Portugal.

from the end of the 16th century became the property of the state after the suppression of religious orders in Portugal in 1834.

A national monument since 2002, the institution went under the name of Palácio das Cortes between 1834 and 1911, after the establishment of the liberal government, Palácio do Congresso between 1911 and 1933, and Palácio da Assembleia Nacional between 1933 and 1974, the date of the Carnation Revolution. In the middle of the 20th century, it was also called Palácio de São Bento, in allusion to the former monastery, and retained this name after 1976, when it became the seat of the Assembleia da República.

During the 19th and 20th centuries, the former monastery was subject to various remodelling projects, which transformed it completely. The rebuilding after the fire in 1895 lasted over 50 years, following the designs of Miguel Ventura Terra, and gave the building the Neoclassical lines visible today.

The external stone staircase was constructed in 1914, to the designs of the architect Cristino da Silva, and has two large stone lions on guard, by the sculptor Raul Xavier. The façade is punctuated by seated allegorical female figures in togas – Prudence, Justice, Strength and Temperance. They are carved in coarse-grained white marble.

The thirteen Corinthian columns and the five windows with perfect semicircular arches are surmounted by a triangular pediment thirty metres long by six metres high and a tympanum decorated by the sculptor Simões de Almeida. It represents the Estado Novo, or New State (the dictatorship's name for itself), with a motto in Latin – "Omnia Pro Patria", "All for the Country" – symbolising the nation. There are another eighteen allegories representing different activities such as trade and industry.

The interior of the building is amply decorated, in particular the main vestibule. It retains the original pink and white marble flooring and the old chapels of the monastery, which were closed and now contain niches with busts of illustrious Portuguese cultural figures, parliamentarians from the time of the monarchy and the First Republic, and important MPs. The bells belonging to São Bento monastery church are also on show.

The grand staircase was designed by the architect António Lino in 1936 and substituted the old monastery stairs. It gives access to eight doors surmounted by triangular pediments with groups of sculpture representing the eight provinces of Portugal of the time and the arms of the main cities where the Cortes (parliament under the kings) met in the country. Historical murals decorate all the walls.

The cloister in the south wing of the palace is situated on the site of one of the four original monastery cloisters. It has semicircular arches and arches with a straight lintel resting on Tuscan pillars, in addition to a garden with four flowerbeds, with their olive trees, and a fountain from the end of the 18th century, with a circular pool.

The Room of the Lost Steps (Sala dos Passos Perdidos) lies immediately at the top of the grand staircase beside the Chamber of Sessions (Sala de Sessões) and represents the central point in the comings and goings of MPs, members of the government and journalists. The barrel vaulted ceiling is painted with allegorical figures by João Vaz and Benvindo Ceia. The pink and white marble walls have eighteen double pilasters and six panels with oil paintings on canvas by the famous Portuguese painter Columbano Bordalo Pinheiro (1857-1929), who belonged to the school of naturalism and realism. The garden at the back of the building forms the boundary with the area of the prime minister's official residence.

The new building of the Assembleia da República was inaugurated in 1999 and extends along Praça de São Bento. It was designed by the architect Fernando Távora, who gave it an aesthetically sober appearance, covering it with square pink and white ashlar masonry. **Rua de São Bento** begins in front of the new wing of the Assembleia da República. It has various antique dealers, as well the residences of two of the icons of Portuguese culture – Alexandre Herculano, the Romantic writer, historian, journalist and poet, and the celebrated fado singer Amália Rodrigues, who died in 1999. **The Amália Rodrigues House Museum (Casa-Museu Amália Rodrigues)** can be found at No. 193.

The world-famous Queen of Fado lived here, where it is still almost possible to breathe in her perfume among her personal possessions – the black fringed shawl, the guitar, the medium grand piano, the pictures, the roses and the wonderful dresses she wore on stage.

She renewed fado by singing the poems of great and famous Portuguese poets – such as Camões and Bocage – as well as of lyricists and poets of her time – Pedro Homem de Mello and David Mourão-Ferreira, among others. Born in 1920, she already sang as a child, though her first triumph would be in the Copacabana Casino in Rio de Janeiro. Her international career began in 1950, when she took part in the performances for the Marshall Plan, through which the USA supported Europe after the war.

From Lisbon to Rio de Janeiro, New York to Rome, Tokyo to the Soviet Union, Mexico to London, and Madrid to Paris, Amália Rodrigues took fado to the whole world. That poignant singing from the Portuguese soul, that perfection of guitars.

THE AMÁLIA RODRIGUES HOUSE MUSEUM (CASA-MUSEU AMÁLIA RODRIGUES)
The former home of the celebrated Portuguese fado singer, in Rua de São Bento.

V. Estrela and Prazeres

Tram 28 now faces a steep climb, **Estrela Road (Calçada da Estrela)**. In the 17th century, this area was just fields, with the walls of the Benedictine monastery on the right. The road took its name from this monastery, dedicated to Our Lady of the Star (Nossa Senhora da Estrela), which the Military Hospital now occupies. It lies close to Estrela Gardens (Jardim da Estrela).

In front of the Assembleia da República there is another garden, the Garden of the Little French Sisters (Jardim das Francesinhas), whose name comes from an old convent established in the area in 1667. In 1935, it was also called the Garden of Old Lisbon (Jardim Lisboa Antiga), when it was the site of an exhibition recreating the old neighbourhoods of Lisbon. Leopoldo Almeida's group of marble sculptures 'The Family', which stands close to the pond and public fountain, was unveiled in 1947. At the top of Calçada da Estrela, the tram 28 reaches another square, Largo da Estrela, with its Romantic garden on one side and the Basilica of Estrela's white façade on the other. The **Jardim da Estrela** is full of mystery – even today the legend persists of an enchanted statue in the lake, Costa Mota's 'The king's daughter guarding ducks'. Also known as the Jardim de Guerra Junqueiro, the garden exists thanks to Baron of Barcelinhos' donations and Queen Maria II's cooperation, which, in 1842, made it possible to prepare and carry out António Bernardo da Costa Cabral's landscape designs.

Designed in the style of the English Romantic movement, this garden was the meeting point of the Lisbon aristocracy until the end of the 19th century. One of its treasures is the wrought iron bandstand, with its ashlar masonry base and Indian motifs in the arch and column designs. It was moved to the garden from the Public Promenade (Passeio Público) in Avenida da Liberdade in 1932.

ESTRELA GARDENS (JARDIM DA ESTRELA)
The prim flowerbeds of a Romantic-age garden; its spreading trees give the impression of a wood in the middle of Lisbon.

Beside the lush vegetation, the walkways tempt the visitor to take a stroll. The charm of the garden is enhanced by the bronze and marble statues honouring famous figures in Portuguese history – for example, Antero de Quental, a 19th-century poet and writer who committed suicide on a garden bench in the Azores in 1891. The garden also has a very popular jewellery and crafts fair on the first weekend of every month, and, in a small kiosk, there is a library that offers sanctuary to those who love reading.

But what catches the visitor's attention most are the decorative flowerbeds and luxuriant trees – mulberry trees, poplars, oaks, chestnut trees, palm trees, cluster pines, plane trees, dragon trees, olive trees, cedars, acacias, araucarias and willows – which turn this garden into a wood, right in the middle of the city. In 1941, its shady trees were replanted after a destructive cyclone.

Opposite the garden, the **Estrela Basilica (Basílica da Estrela)** is a late Baroque monument with Neoclassical features. It has a dome, four columns with decorative capitals, twin towers, and statues of saints and allegorical figures. The church is the mausoleum of Queen Maria I: though she died in Brazil, her Empire-style tomb is in the transept. She is the only queen of the House of Bragança who does not lie with the other kings and queens in the mausoleum in St Vincent de Fora Monastery.

The whole history of Estrela Basilica is connected with Queen Maria I, who, as a princess, made a promise on her wedding day to build this church if she had a son to inherit the throne. When her wish was fulfilled – though her son José, born in 1761, died of smallpox before the church was completed in 1790 – the Queen commissioned the architects of the School of Mafra to build the church, the first in the world dedicated to the Sacred Heart of Jesus.

In the spacious interior, clad with grey, pink and ochre marble from Pêro Pinheiro, Sintra and Cascais, various paintings by Pompeo Batoni are of particular note. An example is the high-altar panel, painted in Rome, which represents an allegory of devotion to the Heart of Jesus, portrayed in the middle of heaven among bright clouds, surrounded by adoring cherubim and seraphim.

The great dome is lit by circles of ox-eye and large vertical windows that shed a delicate light inside the church. The bronzes, the columns, the balustrades, the rostra, the altarpieces, the confessionals and the great chests, inlaid by artists of the time, lend a sense of unparalleled beauty to Estrela Basilica.

The sacristy contains the tomb of the Archbishop of Thessalonica, Brother Inácio de São Caetano, the Queen's confessor, considered the second founder of the adjacent Convent of the Discalced (barefoot) Carmelites of St Teresa. The nativity scene is the work of Machado de Castro (and his followers), who was also responsible for the archbishop's tomb. Other works by his school are the statues of the Mother of Jesus and St Joseph, in the niches in the vestibule to the Basilica, and the façade statues, in particular the figures of Faith, Devotion, Gratitude and Generosity, set above four large columns. Finally, it is worth noting the three large wrought-iron gateways and the bell towers surmounted by contoured pinnacles adorned with Baroque flame sculptures.

Tram 28 now wends its way to **Campo de Ourique**, a neighbourhood in the heart of Lisbon between Amoreiras, Estrela and Prazeres. Though essentially residential, it has elegant shops and traditional cafés with terraces that are always full in summer.

ESTRELA BASILICA (BASÍLICA DA ESTRELA)
The fine bell towers of a church built to fulfil Queen Maria I's promise.

THE INTERIOR OF ESTRELA BASILICA
The elaborate tomb of the Queen of Portugal and the imposing dome, clad in grey, pink and ochre marble.

THE FERNANDO PESSOA HOUSE (CASA FERNANDO PESSOA)
Façade of the Portuguese poet's last home, decorated with lines from the Ode of Ricardo Reis.

Campo de Ourique is also the neighbourhood where the poet Fernando Pessoa spent the last fifteen years of his life. The house, **Casa Fernando Pessoa**, at 16 Rua Coelho da Rocha, is keeping this very great Portuguese-language poet's memory alive.

Opened in 1993, Casa Fernando Pessoa holds part of the poet's estate – objects and furniture, catalogued as municipal property. Fernando Pessoa's bedroom lies on one of the three floors and contains the chest of drawers where, on the night of 8 March 1914 (as he stated himself in a letter of 13 January 1935), he wrote three of his greatest poems – 'O Guardador de Rebanhos', by Alberto Caeiro, 'A Chuva Oblíqua', by Pessoa himself, and 'Ode Triunfal', by Álvaro de Campos.

The library, with different sections, is situated on the ground floor and includes the poet's own library of 1200 volumes. It possesses almost all the publications written by and about Fernando Pessoa and a store of Portuguese and foreign poetry. It also has personal items and documents belonging to the poet, such as the first edition of *Mensagem*, the only book he had published in his lifetime. The objects on display in this room include José de Almada Negreiros' famous portrait of Fernando Pessoa, painted for the café Os Irmãos Unidos in 1954. It was later sold at auction and finally offered to Lisbon City Hall by Jorge de Brito. Other paintings by contemporary artists such as Júlio Pomar, Costa Pinheiro and Renato Cruz, among others, are on display in different rooms, in addition to the projected lampshade, with designs and poems by various artists, including Bertina Lopes, Cruzeiro Seixas and Mário Cesariny.

An auditorium, a garden and various exhibition rooms complete the facilities of Casa Fernando Pessoa, which regularly holds symposia, poetry reading sessions, meetings of national and foreign writers, thematic conferences, workshops, exhibitions of the visual arts and workshops for children. A little of Fernando Pessoa's universe is within everybody's reach – and, if a tourist wishes to see Lisbon through his eyes, Pessoa wrote a book called 'Lisbon: what the tourist should see'. The first edition was only published in 1992.

Back on the Tram 28 route, there are a series of **Art Nouveau buildings** to be admired in Rua Saraiva de Carvalho, in particular the one on the street corner at 131 Rua Ferreira Borges. A commemorative plaque states that "Here, at daybreak on 4 October 1910, the first grenade for the Implantation of the Republic exploded. The heroic regiment Artillery 1 discharged this shell".

Further ahead on the right, still in Rua Saraiva de Carvalho, rises the **Church of the Holy Constable (Igreja do Santo Condestável)**, a neo-Gothic edifice built to the designs of Vasco Morais Palmeiro between 1946 and 1951. It is dedicated to the Holy Constable, who was canonised by Pope Benedict XVI in 2009. This completed a process that began in 1641, when the Cortes (parliament) presented the first beatification request to Pope Urban VIII. The request was renewed over the centuries until, in 1918, Pope Benedict XV confirmed the veneration of the Holy Constable. This Portuguese nobleman and warrior was the strategist of the Portuguese victory over the Spanish at the Battle of Aljubarrota in 1385. Nuno Álvares Pereira, to use his real name, a knight and shield-bearer of Queen Leonor Teles, distinguished himself in the patriotic party that called on João, Master of Avis, to lead the revolt against the Castilians. João, in the meantime King João I, appointed him Constable of the Kingdom in 1385.

CAMPO DE OURIQUE
The various Art Nouveau buildings decorating the streets of this beautiful residential neighbourhood in Lisbon.

CHURCH OF THE HOLY CONSTABLE (IGREJA DO SANTO CONDESTÁVEL)

The neo-Gothic style of the church dedicated to the saint, who was canonised in 2009.

Incredible stained-glass windows by the modern artist Almada Negreiros.

After ensuring Portuguese independence with the victory at Aljubarrota and participating in the conquest of Ceuta in 1415, Nuno Álvares Pereira donated a large part of his property to his family and companions in arms and withdrew to Carmo Monastery (Lisbon) in 1423, where he took the name Friar Nuno de Santa Maria. Even before he died, on Easter Sunday 1431, he was popularly referred to as the Holy Constable.

The whiteness of the plaster on the façade of the Church of the Holy Constable contrasts with the grey fine-pointed Sintra granite. The arms of Portugal's second royal house are set high over the arch of the main entry and there is a group of sculptures portraying the Holy Constable flanked by the Angel of Portugal and the Archangel St Michael in the portico. The building is completed with two towers – the baptistery and bell towers – and the cross of the Pereira arms, on top of the facade.

Inside the church, the impressive fresco by Portela Júnior and Joaquim Rebocho represents the glorification of St Nuno de Santa Maria. The scene includes a choir of angels, the king, the knight and the jurist, in addition to a soldier, a friar, the flags of King João I and Nuno Álvares himself, and the Carmelite banner. The tomb with the relics of the Holy Constable, by Soares Branco, is situated beneath the high altar.

In the transept, the four large stained-glass windows by the modernist painter Almada Negreiros, one of Portugal's most important 20th century artists, are remarkable. On one side, two windows depict the Heart of Mary and the Annunciation by the Angel, under the letters A and M, the first letters of Ave Maria, the angel's greeting to Our Lady. On the other side, there are two more windows with the images of the Heart of Jesus and the Good Shepherd, with the letters alpha and omega, the first and last letters of the Greek alphabet – symbolising God, the beginning and end of all.

As the visitor passes through the avenue alongside the church with its olive trees and cypresses, there is a landscaped square. It has two aged and spreading trees – Tipuanas – and a painted-tile panel by Teresa Corte recounting the history of the parish with notable figures from the neighbourhood, such as Fernando Pessoa.

Tram 28 now draws close to its final stop in Prazeres, as it encircles the St João Bosco roundabout. This is the site of the **Cemetery of Pleasures (Cemitério dos Prazeres)**, the largest in the city, which offers a fine view over the Valley of Alcântara and the river. The name, in fact, is derived from an old estate occupying this area, where the cemetery was installed after an outbreak of cholera in the city in 1833.

The site is considered a veritable open-air museum, a repository of architecture, town planning, sculpture and heraldry in the history of Portugal of its time. A stroll down the wide avenues, under the shady cypresses and jacarandas, reveals a whole range of different attitudes towards death.

The large number of carefully sculptured coats of arms gave rise to a catalogue dedicated to modern funerary heraldry. It is possible to see the arms of noble families from the 1800s and an abundant collection of statues and professional and Masonic symbols. Famous personalities from Portuguese cultural life lie in the artists' section, e.g. the painters Mário Cesariny and Maluda, along with actors, singers, writers and television announcers.

However, the most impressive is the Jazigo Palmela, the largest private mausoleum in Europe and one of the most original

ST. JOÃO BOSCO SQUARE (PRAÇA DE SÃO JOÃO BOSCO)
This roundabout marks the point where Tram 28 arrives and departs in Prazeres.

CEMETERY OF PLEASURES (CEMITÉRIO DOS PRAZERES)
*A real open-air museum of architecture, sculpture and heraldry
in the Portuguese history of its time.*

Portuguese funerary constructions. The space outside reflects the symbolism of a masonic temple and, in the chapel inside, various statues by important sculptors decorate the tombs. These include an extraordinary Carrara-marble low-relief by Canova, which is unique in Portugal, and work by Calmels, as well as work by Teixeira Lopes, one of the greatest Portuguese sculptors from the end of the 19th century, who did not finish the memorial statue for the place that the 3rd Duke of Palmela occupies with his Duchess.

The building was designed by the architect José Cinatti, a Mason. However, he concealed the Masonic symbols as the first Duke of Palmela, who commissioned the building in 1849, was not a Mason. Thus, in allusion to the numbers 7, 5 and 3, perfect numbers in Masonry, the way into the building contains seven steps, with five more for the crypt, and the number three, which mirrors a cosmic dimension in Masonic symbolism and represents the dimension of the indivisible triad, is engraved in the book of the Angel of Death, on top of the mausoleum.

The organisation of the building reflected the Temple of Solomon. So the maidservants buried here occupy the left hand side – the north. This corresponds to the north column of the Temple of Solomon, where the apprentices sat, which is female. On the right-hand side, which corresponds to the south column, the male or solar column, the menservants are buried. In the chapel, situated to the east, the Palmela family are buried.

Barons, earls and marchionesses are also interred in the Cemetery of Prazeres, including the marchionesses of Pombal and Counts Teles de Menezes. The family mausoleums built since the Romantic period are real works of art. Throughout the cemetery, there are signposts indicating the different possible routes and, in the museum unit, there are temporary and permanent exhibitions. They exhibit objects representing Faith, with religious images, Light, with objects to help the deceased negotiate the world of darkness, Flowers, to perfume the space, and Ostentation, with the most magnificent pieces in the collection. Tram 28 comes to the end of its journey opposite Prazeres Cemetery – but also returns along the route day after day, renewing the joy of everyday life in this city as it basks in this radiant and crystalline light. Another tram also starts its journey at this point – the No. 25, to Rua da Alfândega, close to Terreiro do Paço, yet another route full of history through this Lisbon spreading out to the horizon.

VI. The History of Tram 28

Tram 28, which at present travels the 7 km from Prazeres to Graça (and on to Martim Moniz, in the case of its longer itinerary), is the most iconic route in the Carris tram line network in Lisbon. Since the line was opened in 1914, between Praça Luís de Camões and Estrela, this line has included some of the most beautiful scenes in the city.

During the first part of the 20th century, Tram 28 steadily lengthened its route through the hills of Lisbon, initially to travel on to Rossio, in 1928, when it became known as Line 28 Rossio-Estrela. Four years later, an additional line appeared, No. 28 A, from Rua da Conceição, in Baixa, to Prazeres. It was only in 1973 that Tram 28 started to cover the long stretch to Graca, becoming one of the symbols of Lisbon. It attracted a growing number of tourists who were enchanted by the driver's skill in negotiating the tight bends and narrow streets presented by certain neighbourhoods. In 1984, the line was extended again, from Graça to Martin Moniz, following the suppression of other lines and the expansion of the service with Line 28 B. This ran from Martim Moniz to Rua da Conceição, though it was also extended later to Estrela. Five years afterwards, a turning circle was installed in Praça Luís de Camões, a kind of terminus that eliminated the need for the tram to reverse. This system would also be installed at Estrela and Prazeres (Praça de São João Bosco), where the line terminated.

Thus, the characteristic Maley & Taunton two-way 700 Series trams, with two 45 hp motors (i.e. 90 hp) and manual compressed air, electromagnetic and electropneumatic brakes, travelled the hills of Lisbon with their unmistakable coat of yellow paint and the constant ping-ping of the bell.

CARRIS MUSEUM (MUSEU DA CARRIS)
A miniature of the old Lisbon trams.

Tram 28 covers the Prazeres-Martim Moniz route, via Graça, though at certain times it only covers the Prazeres-Graça or Estrela-Graça sections – the most beautiful and most interesting. It usually leaves every 15 minutes and takes between 40 minutes and an hour to complete the trip, depending on the vicissitudes of the motor traffic on the way.

Single tickets may be bought on board, though there are various ticket types available for tourists at the metro stations and kiosks in the city. The cards *Cartão 7 Colinas* and *Viva Viagem* may be inexpensively topped up with single or combined journeys – Metro 24h and Carris (buses, trams and elevators) – at ticket machines in the metro stations. There is also the *Zapping* card – a multimodal ticket valid on Carris (buses, trams and elevators), the metro and Calcilhas ferries (cacilheiros). Finally, there is the *Lisboa Card*, issued by the Lisbon Tourist Association and sold at tourist offices. In the summer, Tram 28 operates from 6.20 in the morning to 23.20 on working days, from 6.15 to 23.05 on Saturdays and from 7.25 to 23.05 on Sundays and public holidays.

Line 28 has over 45 trams available. They have been restored and modernised, though retaining their traditional lines, with their wooden bodywork and iron chassis. These were rebuilt in the Carris workshops, with AEG/Ferrostaal bogies. The trams are 8.38 m long, 2.37 m wide and 3.19 m high and can carry 20 seated and 38 standing passengers.

With its two 600 V DC motors, Tram 28 reaches a maximum speed of 50 km/h. Articulated trams allow brake energy recovery and the return of this energy to the network for consumption by other vehicles, such as Tram 28. The energy recovered represents around 30% of the energy consumed by articulated trams.

On the 7 km journey through the city, the tram driver skilfully manipulates the control panel, which includes the driver's valve (a manual compressed air brake), a geostatic brake with the driving handle that controls the speed from power points (parallel and in series), and the electromagnetic brake on the rail.

In addition to all the control items on the panel – for lights, doors, air pressure, points, rail brake etc – there is a GPS system that allows any of the trams in the fleet to be localised along its route, along with a radio system for communication with headquarters. Line 28's overhead network, which is fixed and uncompensated, is only prepared for trams with a trolley pole and pulley, as it is physically impossible for vehicles with pantographs to travel on this stretch of the network, given the closeness of the verandas in some of the narrow streets along the way.

Carris, a company that originated in Brazil

In 1872, in Rio de Janeiro, Brazil, the writer Luciano Cordeiro de Sousa and his diplomat brother Francisco established the Lisbon Railway Company (Companhia Carris de Ferro de Lisboa), a company that planned to provide the Portuguese capital with an American-style transport system – horse-drawn carriages on rails. After receiving authorisation from Portugal in the same year, the company installed itself in Lisbon the next year and, in 1873, opened the first line of "Americanos", on a route between Santa

Apolónia, the railway station for the north and east, and Santos, on the western edge of the city.

The next year, the Santo Amaro depot was established on the lands of the former Quinta do Saldanha, where the company started to build stables for the 421 head of livestock, carriage sheds, workshops and barns, in addition to the areas for the 54 carriages in operation. Today, these large premises house the Carris Museum (Museu da Carris), with a collection that contains, in particular, three nuclei recounting the company's 137-year history.

The main building contains showcases with documents of the company's most notable moments and models of trams, buses and lifts. The visit proceeds on board an electric tram from the museum's collection – a model with red curtains, velvet-upholstered seating and lights hanging from the padded ceiling. It takes the visitors to two bays with a collection of vehicles and replicas – evolving from animal traction to electric traction – that were in service between the late 19th century and the late 1940s.

The itinerary continues chronologically in Bay 2, which displays the reconstruction of a sub-depot and a workshop with all their equipment and another series of models of trams and buses dating from the fifties to the present, all in perfect working condition.

In Carris' long history, there have been important events for the transport system in the capital, such as the installation of elevators at different points in the city, even in the 19th century. Examples are the Lavra, Bica and Glória elevators, which used water in hydraulic counterweight systems and then steam for the tractive effort, before being electrified in the early 20th century. The iconic Elevator of Santa Justa was steam-driven when it came into service in 1902. It was only much later that Carris acquired it.

The electric traction system using overhead conductors was installed on all Carris network cars in 1897, with the company obtaining exclusive use of the system. In 1901, the tramcar service was introduced. Another depot, this time in Amoreiras, was built for tramcar services in 1937.

In 1940, for the Exhibition of the Portuguese World in Belém, Carris purchased six AEC Regent Mk II buses and, four years later, the city bus service was officially inaugurated. A few years later, in 1947, the first double-decker buses arrived, and where in use during several decades. The bus fleet was renewed in 1974 and another 200 vehicles were put into service.

In the 1990s, new medium-sized buses began to operate in the city, especially on the more tortuous routes in the city. In 1991, twenty new articulated buses equipped with turbo motors and intercoolers went into service as part of the plan to modernise the fleet. They are efficient, use less fuel and pollute less.

Micro-buses were introduced in 1993 and, in 1995, the first 10 rapid transit trams were introduced on the line to Belém along the river. A little later, Carris completed the remodelling of 45 traditional trams, retaining the historical outside appearance and improving their performance in terms of speed, security and noise.

Historical documents of the Lisbon Railway Company (Companhia Carris de Ferro de Lisboa), established in Brazil in 1872, and a collection of trams and buses from the last 100 years.

Destination banners from old Lisbon trams and buses.

The Carris Museum (Museu da Carris) opened in 1999 in various historical buildings in the Santa Amaro depot, the company's first depot in Lisbon. In the first years of the new century, natural gas powered buses were introduced, in a project involving efficient energy use. In addition, in 2002, the Elevators of Lavra, Glória, Bica and Santa Justa were classified as national monuments.

In 2004, the new contactless ticketing system began to operate, with the adoption of the *Lisboa Viva* card for season tickets and the *7 Colinas* card for other tickets. The fleet renewal process also began with the purchase of 408 new buses in three years. The company's headquarters and all central services moved to the Miraflores Complex in 2005 and, the next year, Carris was awarded Quality Management System certification – the first Portuguese public transport operator to receive overall certification.

The first model of a closed tram, operating in Lisbon from 1901.

NYSSE ARRUDA

A Brazilian journalist based in Lisbon for 20 years; she has written three books on sailing, her specialist field, for which she has covered various round-the-world regattas, ocean crossings and world championships as a professional journalist. This has included participation in an Antarctica expedition on board the Brazilian Navy icebreaker Barão de Teffé in 1986, and the Grand Regatta Columbus 92, on board the Polish tall ship Dar Mlodziezi, from Lisbon to Puerto Rico.

Nysse Arruda has worked with various Portuguese publications – magazines such as *Rotas & Destinos*, *Vela & Náutica*, *Ideias & Negócios*, *Preguiça*, *Única*, *Pública* and *Fugas* and newspapers such as *Público*, *Jornal de Negócios*, *Correio do Brasil*, *Expresso* and *Diário de Notícias*. She has also written travel articles and profiles of perso-nalities in the cultural world and was the author of the first *Guia de Luxo de Lisboa-Sucre Collection*, in 2006.

In São Paulo, Brazil, where she began her career as a journalist, she wrote for the newspapers *Folha de S. Paulo*, *Estado de S. Paulo* and *Jornal da Tarde* and wrote the first book in Portuguese on the Whitbread Round the World Race 1989-90, which was published by Editora Brasiliense and sponsored by the Ford company and the businessman and sailor Eduardo Souza Ramos. Since then, she has covered five editions of this sailing event, at present known as the Volvo Ocean Race. She also closely followed the four years' preparation for the sailor Amyr Klink's project "Primeira Invernagem Solitária na Antárctica" (1st Solo Over-wintering in Antarctica), in 1989-90.

HENRIQUE CAYATTE

A designer and illustrator with a vast corpus in the publishing area. Founder and author of design global, editor and illustrator of the newspaper *Público* until 2000. Co-author of the EXPO '98 sign and communication system. Responsible for the design of the Portugal Pavilions in the universal expositions Expo'98, Hannover 2000, and Aichi 2005 in Japan. Commissioner and designer for exhibitions such as Cassiano Branco – uma obra para o futuro, Liberdade e Cidadania – 100 Anos Portugueses, Engenharia Portuguesa do Século XX, and 1990/2004 Arquitectura e Design de Portugal at the Milan Triennial.

Creator of the design of the magazine *Egoísta*, the newspaper *Diário de Notícias* [until February 2007] and the magazine *Cubo*, among other publications. Creator of the overall design of the new Portuguese electronic passport and the single card for the citizen. Elected as a member of the European management of design [BEDA - The Bureau of European Design Associations]. Guest lecturer at Aveiro University. President of the Centro Português de Design. Designer responsible for the Centenary Celebrations of the Portuguese Republic.

CLARA AZEVEDO

A freelance photographer and founder of Clara Azevedo Produções Fotográficas Lda., Clara Azevedo began her career with the Associated Press and the newspaper *Expresso*, between 1987 and 1995. She was advisor to the ARCO Photography Department in 1988 and was also invited by the F-Stop Gallery of Somerset Development and Tourism Council to carry out a photographic project on the Roman baths in the city of Bath and hold a workshop for the photography students at Trowbridge College. Since 1998, she has been creating and producing photographs and projects for the publishing field and has a publishing record that includes such work as *Termas Portuguesas*, *Jorge Sampaio*, *Retratos de uma Vitória*, *Splendid Isolation – O Mito do Grande Hotel*, Roma, with a text by António Mega Ferreira, in addition to ten guides in the series *Essencial – O seu guia alternativo de viagens* (Your alternative travel book) and the book *Doce Lisboa, guias e receitas das melhores pastelarias*, (Sweet Lisbon, guide and best pastry shops' recipes).

Clara Azevedo has held various individual exhibitions in Galeria Diferença in Lisbon and Círculo das Artes Plásticas in Coimbra, Centro Cultural del Reloj (part of the Madrid Capital of Culture 1992 programme), Museu da Imagem de Braga, Fundação Luso- -Brasileira and Centro de Artes e Espectáculos, in Figueira da Foz. She has also taken part in various collective exhibitions in Lisbon, Beja and Mitra and, abroad, in London, Paris, Greece and the United States.

ELÉCTRICO 28

STOPS

ESTRELA/PRAZERES

- Largo Martim Moniz
- Rua da Palma
- Igreja dos Anjos
- Rua Maria Andrade
- Rua Maria da Fonte
- Rua Angelina Vidal
- Sapadores
- Rua da Graça
- Largo da Graça
- Rua Voz do Operário
- Calçada de São Vicente
- Rua das Escolas Gerais
- Largo das Portas do Sol
- Miradouro de Santa Luzia
- Limoeiro
- Sé
- Largo de Santo António
- Rua da Conceição
- Calçada de São Francisco
- Largo de Belas-Artes
- Rua Vítor Cordon/Rua Serpa Pinto
- Rua Duques de Bragança
- Chiado
- Praça Luís de Camões
- Calhariz (Bica)
- Santa Catarina
- Calçada do Combro
- Largo Dr. António de Sousa de Macedo
- Rua Poiais de São Bento/Rua Poço dos Negros
- Rua de São Bento
- Calçada da Estrela
- Estrela (Basílica e Jardim)
- Rua Domingos Sequeira
- Rua Saraiva de Carvalho (Campo de Ourique)
- Igreja do Santo Condestável
- Prazeres

GRAÇA/MARTIM MONIZ

- Prazeres
- Igreja do Santo Condestável
- Rua Saraiva de Carvalho (Campo de Ourique)
- Rua Domingos Sequeira
- Estrela (Basílica e Jardim)
- Calçada da Estrela
- Rua de São Bento
- Rua Poiais de São Bento/Rua Poço dos Negros
- Largo Dr. António de Sousa de Macedo
- Calçada do Combro
- Santa Catarina
- Calhariz (Bica)
- Praça Luís de Camões
- Chiado
- Rua Duques de Bragança
- Rua Vítor Cordon/Rua Serpa Pinto
- Largo de Belas-Artes
- Calçada de São Francisco
- Rua da Conceição
- Largo de Santo António
- Sé
- Limoeiro
- Miradouro de Santa Luzia
- Largo das Portas do Sol
- Rua das Escolas Gerais
- Calçada de São Vicente
- Rua Voz do Operário
- Largo da Graça
- Rua da Graça
- Sapadores
- Rua Angelina Vidal
- Rua Maria da Fonte
- Rua Maria Andrade
- Igreja dos Anjos
- Rua da Palma
- Largo Martim Moniz

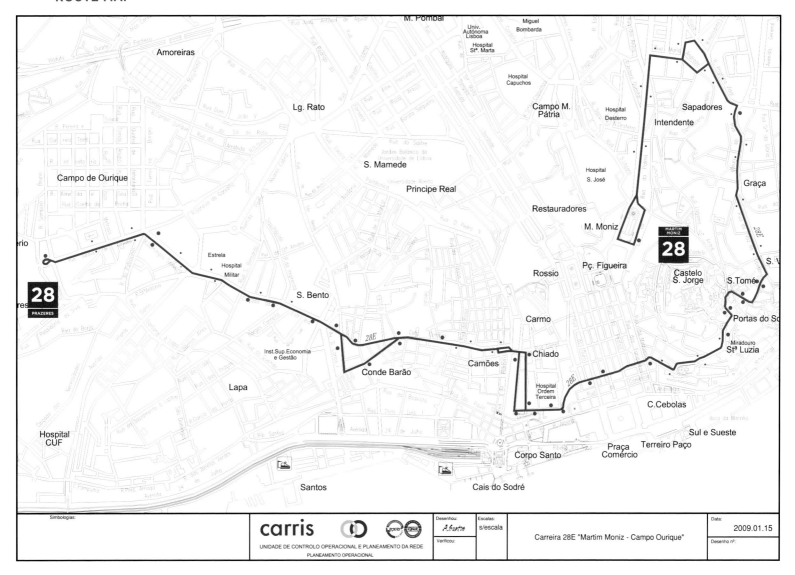

ELÉCTRICO 28
ROUTE MAP

M. Pombal
Univ. Autónoma Lisboa
Miguel Bombarda
Hospital Stª. Marta
Amoreiras
Hospital Capuchos
Campo M. Pátria
Sapadores
Hospital Desterro
Intendente
Lg. Rato
Graça
S. Mamede
Jardim Botânico da Universidade de Lisboa
Hospital S. José
Principe Real
Campo de Ourique
Restauradores
M. Moniz
MARTIM MONIZ
28
Estrela
Hospital Militar
Pç. Figueira
Rossio
Castelo S. Jorge
S.Tomé
28 PRAZERES
S. Bento
Carmo
Portas do So
28E
Miradouro Stª Luzia
Inst.Sup.Economia e Gestão
Chiado
Camões
Conde Barão
Lapa
Hospital Ordem Terceira
28E
C.Cebolas
Hospital CUF
Sul e Sueste
Corpo Santo
Praça Comércio
Terreiro Paço
Santos
Cais do Sodré

carris
UNIDADE DE CONTROLO OPERACIONAL E PLANEAMENTO DA REDE
PLANEAMENTO OPERACIONAL
Desenhou: A.Santos
Verificou:
Escalas: s/escala
Carreira 28E "Martim Moniz - Campo Ourique"
Data: 2009.01.15
Desenho nº:

ELÉCTRICO 28

INDEX OF MONUMENTS

FROM BAIXA TO GRAÇA

MILLENNIUM BCP
ARCHAEOLOGICAL
NUCLEUS
NÚCLEO ARQUEOLÓGICO
MILLENNIUM BCP
Rua dos Correeiros, 9 r/c
Tel. 211 131 004
Thursday 3-5 pm
Sat 10 am-1 pm and 3-5 pm
In 2010 the site may be open
every day.

MUDE – MUSEUM OF
DESIGN AND FASHION
MUDE – MUSEU
DO DESIGN E DA MODA
Rua Augusta, 24
Tel. 218 886 117
Tues-Sun 10 am-8 pm
Fri and Sat 10 am-10 pm

CAFÉ-RESTAURANTE
MARTINHO DA ARCADA
Praça do Comércio, 3
Tel. 218 879 259
Mon-Sat
12 noon-4 pm and 7-11 pm
Closed on Sundays

CHURCH OF
MARY MAGDALENE
IGREJA DA MADALENA
Largo da Madalena, 1
Tel. 218 870 987
Mon-Sat 8 am-6 pm
Sunday 9 am-12 noon

CHURCH AND MUSEUM
OF ST ANTHONY
IGREJA E MUSEU
DE SANTO ANTÓNIO
Largo de Santo António
da Sé
Tel. 218 869 145
Every day 9 am-7 pm

LISBON PATRIARCHAL
CATHEDRAL
SÉ PATRIARCAL
DE LISBOA
Largo da Sé
Tel. 218 886 752
Every day 9 am-5 pm

PUBLIC CONVENIENCES
AT THE CATHEDRAL
CASAS DE BANHO
PÚBLICAS À SÉ
(Pre-Pombaline ruins
– Ruínas pré-pombalinas)
Largo da Sé
Mon-Sat 9 am-12 noon
and 2-6 pm

ST GEORGE'S CASTLE
CASTELO DE SÃO JORGE
Tel. 218 800 620
Every day 9 am-6 pm

ST LUZIA'S CHURCH
IGREJA DE SANTA LUZIA
Largo de Santa Luzia
Tel. 218 881 303
Tues-Sun 2-6 pm

MUSEUM OF THE
ROMAN THEATRE
MUSEU DO
TEATRO ROMANO
Pátio do Aljube, 5
Tel. 218 820 320
Tues-Sun
10 am-1 pm and 2-6 pm
Closed Mon and public
holidays

RICARDO DO ESPÍRITO
SANTO SILVA FOUNDATION
FUNDAÇÃO RICARDO
DO ESPÍRITO SANTO SILVA
Largo das Portas do Sol, 2
Tel. 218 881 991
Tues-Sun 10 am-5 pm

CHURCH AND MONASTERY
OF SÃO VICENTE DE FORA
IGREJA E MOSTEIRO
DE SÃO VICENTE DE FORA
Largo de São Vicente
Tel. 218 885 652
Tues-Sun 10 am-6 pm

FLEA MARKET
FEIRA DA LADRA
Campo de Santa Clara
Tel. 218 170 800
Tues and Sat 6 am-6 pm

CHURCH OF SANTA
ENGRÁCIA – NATIONAL
MAUSOLEUM
IGREJA DE SANTA
ENGRÁCIA – PANTEÃO
NACIONAL
Campo de Santa Clara
Tel. 218 854 820
Tues-Sun 10 am-5pm

GRAÇA CHURCH
IGREJA DA GRAÇA
Largo da Graça
Tel. 21 887 39 43
Tues-Fri
9:30 am-12:30 pm
and 3-6 pm
Saturday
9:30 am-12:30 pm
and 3-7 pm
Sunday
9:30 am-1 pm
and 5-8 pm

CHAPEL OF OUR LADY
OF THE MOUNT
CAPELA DE NOSSA
SENHORA DO MONTE
Miradouro
Senhora do Monte
Tel. 21 886 9856
Tues-Sat 3 pm-6 pm

CHAPEL OF OUR LADY
OF HEALTH
CAPELA NOSSA SENHORA
DA SAÚDE
Largo Martim Moniz
Mon-Fri 8:45 am-6 pm
Saturday
8:45 am-1 pm and 3-6 pm
Sundays and
public holidays
8:45 am-12 noon

FROM BAIXA TO PRAZERES

LISBON CITY HALL
CÂMARA MUNICIPAL
DE LISBOA
Paços do Concelho
Praça do Município
Tel. 213 236 200

CAFÉ A BRASILEIRA
Rua Garrett, 120-122
Tel. 213 469 541
Every day 8 am-1 am

PASTELARIA BÉNARD
Rua Garrett, 104
Tel. 21 347 31 33
Mon-Sat 8 am-11 pm

**CARMO RUINS AND
ARCHAEOLOGICAL
MUSEUM**
RUÍNAS E MUSEU
ARQUEOLÓGICO
DO CARMO
Largo do Carmo
Tel. 213 478 629
Mon-Sat 10 am-5pm

SANTA JUSTA ELEVATOR
ELEVADOR
DE SANTA JUSTA
Between Rua do Ouro
and Largo do Carmo
Every day 7 am-11 pm
(summer timetable)

BASILICA OF THE MARTYRS
BASÍLICA DOS MÁRTIRES
Rua Garrett, 19
Tel. 213 462 465
Mon-Fri 9 am-7 pm
Sat and Sun 10 am-8 pm

**CHIADO MUSEUM
NATIONAL MUSEUM
OF CONTEMPORARY ART**
MUSEU DO CHIADO
MUSEU NACIONAL DE
ARTE CONTEMPORÂNEA
Rua Serpa Pinto, 4-6
Tel. 213 011 675
Tues-Sun 10 am-6 pm
Free entry on Sunday
until 2 pm

**CHURCH OF OUR LADY
OF LORETO – CHURCH
OF THE ITALIANS**
IGREJA DE NOSSA
SENHORA DO LORETO
(IGREJA DOS ITALIANOS)
Rua da Misericórdia, 2
Tel. 213 423 655
Every day
8 am-12:30 pm and 3-8 pm
Every day
8 am-12:30 pm and 3-8 pm

**CHURCH OF OUR LADY
OF ENCARNATION**
IGREJA DE
NOSSA SENHORA
DA ENCARNAÇÃO
Largo do Chiado, 15
Tel. 213 424 623
Mon-Fri
7:20-11 am and 5-8 pm
Sat and Sun
8:30-11 am and 5-8 pm

**CHURCH AND MUSEUM
OF ST ROQUE**
IGREJA E MUSEU
DE SÃO ROQUE
Largo Trindade Coelho
Tel. 213 235 065
Tues-Sun 9 am-6 pm
Mon 2-6 pm
Thurs 9 am-9 pm

**SÃO LUIZ MUNICIPAL
THEATRE**
TEATRO MUNICIPAL
SÃO LUIZ
Rua António Maria
Cardoso, 38
Tel. 213 257 640
www.teatrosaoluiz.pt

**NATIONAL THEATRE
OF SÃO CARLOS**
TEATRO NACIONAL
DE SÃO CARLOS
Largo de São Carlos
Tel. 213 253 045
www.saocarlos.pt

REFRESHMENT KIOSK
QUIOSQUE DE REFRESCO
LARGO CAMÕES
Praça de Camões
Every day 7 am-1 am

BICA ELEVATOR
ELEVADOR DA BICA
Every day 7 am-10:45 pm

CHURCH OF ST CATHERINE
IGREJA DE SANTA CATARINA
(IGREJA DOS PAULISTAS)
Calçada do Combro
Tel. 213 464 443
Mon-Sat
8:30 am-12:30 pm
and 3-7 pm
Sun 8:30 am-1 pm

**CHURCH OF OUR LADY
OF MERCIES**
IGREJA DE NOSSA
SENHORA DAS MERCÊS
Largo de Jesus
Tel. 213 460 897
Tues-Sun
11 am-1 pm and 5-7 pm
Closed on Monday

**ASSEMBLY OF THE
REPUBLIC (PORTUGUESE
PARLIAMENT)**
PALÁCIO DE SÃO BENTO
ASSEMBLEIA DA
REPÚBLICA
Rua de São Bento
Tel. 213 919 625
Pre-arranged visits only

**AMÁLIA RODRIGUES
HOUSE MUSEUM**
CASA-MUSEU
AMÁLIA RODRIGUES
Rua de São Bento, 193
Tues-Sun 10 am-6 pm

ESTRELA GARDENS
JARDIM DA ESTRELA
Largo da Estrela
Every day 7 am-midnight

ESTRELA BASILICA
BASÍLICA DA ESTRELA
Largo da Estrela
Tel. 213 960 915
Every day 8 am-8 pm
No visits during worship.

**THE FERNANDO
PESSOA HOUSE**
CASA FERNANDO PESSOA
Rua Coelho da Rocha, 16
Tel. 213 913 270
Mon-Sat 10 am-6 pm

**CHURCH OF THE
HOLY CONSTABLE**
IGREJA DO
SANTO CONDESTÁVEL
Rua Saraiva de Carvalho,
Tel. 21 396 53 94
Every day
8 am-1 pm and 4-7:30 pm

PLEASURES CEMETERY
CEMITÉRIO
DOS PRAZERES
Praça de São João Bosco
Tel. 213 912 699
Every day 9 am-5:30 pm
*Guided visits (minimum 4 people)
arranged via e-mail
dgc@cm-lisboa.pt,
or fax: 218 172 817*